AMV

Studio Recording for Musicians.

Studio Recording for Musicians

by Fred Miller

Amsco Publications
New York/London/Sydney

Thanks to Gotham Audio Corporation, New York City, for permission to use photos
of Neumann Microphones, p.19 and 20. Many thanks to Masterdisk Studios, New York City,
Sound Heights Studio, Brooklyn, New York, and Vanguard Records, New York, for giving us
time in their studios for photographing the recording equipment in this book.

Cover design: Pearce Marchbank
Cover photography: George Taylor, Rembrandt Brothers
Book design: Dudley Thomas
Text photographs by Isabelle Francais
Edited by June Wolfberg and Jonathan Firstenberg

Order No. AM 32681
US International Standard Book Number: 0.8256.4204.3
UK International Standard Book Number: 0.7119.0215.1
Library of Congress Catalog Card Number: 80-68647

Exclusive Distributors:
Music Sales Corporation
225 Park Avenue South, New York, NY 10003 USA
Music Sales Limited
8/9 Frith Street, London W1V 5TZ England
Music Sales Pty. Limited
120 Rothschild Street, Rosebery, Sydney, NSW 2018, Australia

Printed in the United States of America by
Vicks Lithograph and Printing Corporation

This book is dedicated to my mother, who made it all possible. . . and to my daughter, who makes it all worthwhile.

Acknowledgments

My thanks to Peter Pickow, June Wolfberg, Jason Shulman, Mike Bieber, and Gil Goldstein for their support in getting this book into your hands. And too, to the following engineers whose experience and craftsmanship have influenced my attitudes and techniques in the recording business: George Massenburg, George Semkiw, Kerry McNabb, Phil Ramone, Vicki Fabry, Lew Hahn, Jeff Zaraya, Harry Munz, Jerry Kornbluth, Harvey Goldberg, Vince Traina, Noel Smith, and Frank Laico. Special thanks to Hank O'Neal, who provided me with unlimited opportunities to find my own way.

Introduction

Chances are that you're a person who works in a recording studio from time to time or would like to do so very soon. Perhaps you're interested in engineering, producing, or arranging for records. Or perhaps you're a musician who has occasion to spend time in studios. If you fit any of these descriptions, this book is written for you. You've either experienced or heard about the special atmosphere that develops in recording studios, and may be wondering what makes it happen. With something as high-pressure, expensive, creative, and potentially rewarding as the recording situation, we all need a certain amount of information to be comfortable. My aim here is to impart a whole lot of that information to you, so that your experience will be a positive one.

This book will guide you through every important step in the recording process, keeping you informed of the goals and requirements of all studio personnel along the way—from the producer to the 14th violinist. Without dwelling on technical criteria, it will make you aware of the things you'll want to know. For example, there will be no need to discuss impendances or resistor values here, because the engineering staff will have those factors under control; but it won't hurt you to know about calibration tones on a master tape, tape speeds, equalization, and decay time of a reverberation chamber.

Chapters deal with specific areas of the recording process, but as all the areas are at least somewhat connected to each other, some overlapping of information will take place. An extensive glosssary of terms is included at the back of the book, should you run across something that sounds like a foreign language.

Throughout the book, I've named specific pieces of equipment found in studios, and in some cases actually recommended some of them. It should be pointed out that engineering is a very personal craft, and different engineers have different preferences for mikes, speakers, drums, digital delay lines, or grand pianos. While the brand names and model numbers mentioned in this book are common, there are other products which have performed well for many engineers and producers. All recommendations are based on my personal experience, but remember that one man's ceiling is another man's floor.

Making records can be a rough road. Failures in communication and human relations can sabotage even a great song, or destroy what might have been a success. This book won't help you write hits or win the hearts of record company A&R people; but if it makes it a little easier to get the sound in your head onto the tape without too much anxiety or confusion, or if it turns you on to some possibilities for enhancing your ideas, then it was worth the writing. May all your records be gold.

—Fred Miller

Contents

Participants in a Recording

Any recording session has several people involved, and each is necessary to fulfill specific functions. While roles may sometimes overlap, and, for example, a musician may produce his own record, the jobs are clearly different enough for individual discussion.

THE PRODUCER

The producer is in charge of all that goes on in the studio during a recording. He or she decides which studio will be used, which musicians, engineers, arrangers, songs, and even artists will make the record. He is responsible for the ultimate sound of the master tape or record. The embodiment of the phrase, "the buck stops here," the producer has the final say in all matters.

He may work for the A&R department of a record company, or he may be an independent producer, making records for ultimate sale to a label or for his own label. The producer's job consists of organizing all the details of a session, from selecting material to be recorded to supervising the mixing process. He may also file musicians' employment contracts, play maracas, make coffee, pay for cabs, call for food, calm down a nervous vocalist, or haul electric

Producer Marcus Barone mixing a disco album for Vanguard Records.

pianos around in the back of his car. Most of all, the producer must create an atmosphere in which the artists can realize their creative potential and get the best performance possible of the material being recorded. He has to be organized, level-headed, diplomatic, musical, efficient, and talented. Producing records is among the most difficult jobs that exist anywhere. But when it's well done, the producer is truly rewarded, both emotionally and professionally.

THE RECORDING ENGINEER

The recording engineer is the liaison between the producer and the machinery. He or she will see that the studio is ready before the session, with all the instruments ready to be played, all or most of the microphones approximately in position, headsets available, machines aligned, and lights adjusted. Most often, the engineer works for the studio and is assigned to a particular project. Frequently, however, a producer may request a specific engineer, having had good experience with him in the past, or having heard good things about him from other producers or musicians. Engineers sometimes work independently, or freelance, and are available for hire in addition to the studio rate or for a percentage of the studio billing. A well-known freelance engineer is often involved in a project even before the studio is selected, and will be asked to recommend studios with the most suitable atmosphere, equipment, and location for the project.

The recording engineer routinely deals with requests like getting a "fat" sound on a bass, creating more of a "shine" on the cymbals, making a trumpet section sound "punchier," and giving a vocal some "depth." He knows how to interpret requests presented in English, musical language, sign language, or even a series of frantic gestures.

Combined with an extensive battery of tools including potentiometers, microphones, equalizers, echo chambers, limiters, and a thousand other devices, the engineer can get you the sound that you want, and the sound that serves the needs of the producer.

Most engineers survive in the business because they're willing and able to please clients. They'll go out of their way to help you get a sound and share your joy if a project sounds good. Your working relationship with your engineer is critical; he can be the make or break point of a recording. In the studio more than any producer or musician, he knows the routines and he is not to be abused. This is not to say that an engineer should be permitted any creative "whim," but in general, you should give him enough time to get a good basic sound or set up an effect you've requested. If he's involved in a procedure and you're edgy about the time, ask him to keep you posted about what's going on. He's working as quickly as he can.

The best engineers know a lot about music. They're aware of where the bridge is in a song, or where the double time starts, and can run the tape to that point without any help. They also know enough about the operation of the studio so that they can replace a bad cord or change a module in the console within a minute or so. They can feel when it's time for a break, when you've been mixing too long and can't hear it anymore. And they know what sounds best in most situations. For example, if your stack of Marshalls sound great in a concert hall but the engineer suggests you record with an old Fender Twin, he has his reasons. And you can be fairly sure that he'll make the Fender sound as close as possible to the stack of Marshalls and still get a good sound on the drums—without peeling the paint off the walls of the studio.

I have, on the other hand, seen inexperienced engineers make what I consider to be unreasonable requests. One such request is to "play louder." When more intensity of sound is desired, playing louder is perfectly in order. But the engineer should not make that response to a request to a musician to turn up

the volume in the headset. Another request is sometimes made for a bassist or even a guitarist to turn off the speakers on his amp. While the absence of sound from the speaker makes life easier for the engineer (because it minimizes leakage from the amp into the piano and drum mikes), it sometimes spoils the "feel of the instrument" for the bassist or guitarist who doesn't have his amp on right next to him. This debate is often best handled by compromise: turn the amp down a bit and, perhaps, put up a couple of gobos. (Gobos are sound baffles placed around amplifiers or individual instruments.)

THE ASSISTANT ENGINEER

Also called "apprentices," "standbys," "juniors," or "seconds," the assistant engineer is usually an engineer-in-training who is there to learn about recording before he or she is actually permitted to run a recording session. In addition to having to soak up knowledge without detailed explanations, he keeps a log of takes, starts and stops the recorders, runs out to the studio to change cables, tests microphones, empties ashtrays, answers the phone, orders lunch, and keeps quiet throughout the session. He's paid amazingly little for this job, but usually considers it a privilege to even be permitted to be there. A very good assistant hustles a lot. He may set up all the mikes before the engineer arrives, having tested them to see that they work. He may have set up a cue balance, or at least a rough one based on previous experience. He will have personally tried on each headset to make sure that it works. He will have set up music stands, sharpened pencils, and otherwise ascertained that everything is in good order when the engineer arrives. The trouble with good assistants is that they quickly become recording engineers, and then the studio needs to get another raw trainee. But this is the nature of the business, and because recording is so magical to so many, trainees are very easy to find.

THE MAINTENANCE ENGINEER

The maintenance engineer has done most all of his work before you arrive. He has aligned all of the tape recorders to be used for the recording. He's made sure that calibration tones appear at the beginning of the first reel of tape, so that if the tape moves to another studio (for overdubs or mixing) its maintenance engineer can make the next tape recorder sound exactly like the first one. He's gone over every piece of equipment and patch cord in the control room at one time or another, to ensure that all perform "up to specs," (or as well as they were intended to perform by the manufacturers). Should something go wrong with a piece of equipment during your session, the engineer will call the maintenance department, and the maintenance engineer will appear quickly to try to solve the problem. You will not be charged for the "down time" it takes him to make

Engineer Jonathan Thayer—One of New York's finest.

Typical seating arrangement for two guitars and bass. Amps are placed behind the gobos.

the room work again, so don't rush him. Your musicians may be expensive, so use the time to rehearse the next song, go over some fine points you needed to mention anyway, or take a break. (Obviously, if a studio has lots of down time and technical problems, think twice about recording a 40-piece string overdub there next time.)

But recording studio maintenance engineers are another breed of cat. Theirs is truly another world and they are fascinating to talk to. They are frequently involved with music or computers or true high-fidelity sound, and have a handle on the nature of technical systems that is unusual in the music business. They know more than you care to hear about the equipment you're working with, and are good folks to know.

THE STUDIO MUSICIAN

The studio musician is a professional sideman. He or she can usually read anything on music paper, and is hired for his ability to read and perform accurately, quickly, and the way you want to hear it. Studio musicians have a vast wealth of information, are up on the latest sounds and licks, and can give them to you at the drop of a hat. Everyone (almost) uses studio musicians in making records . . . from Carly Simon to Blondie. It is common even among artists with terrific bands of their own to pass them over for studio players on a recording, because they are more familiar with the procedures in the studio, they work very efficiently, and their names are impressive on the record jacket.

Almost all musicians hate being called studio musicians. Most of them do, in fact, have musical interests beyond playing in your song or jingle. Randy Brecker is one example. Randy is a highly qualified

studio musician who pursues an active career as a jazz player. He is among the most desirable trumpet/flugelhorn players to have on any jazz date, is a lyrical and swinging composer, and can arrange for a horn section as well as many top "arrangers." He also has a band with his brother Michael, the Brecker Brothers Band, which is a successful recording act in its own right. But hire him to play a C-major scale, and he's right there with all you want and more. His is the kind of professionalism that makes great studio musicians great.

Some good things about studio musicians:
- They can read anything . . . quickly.
- They show up on time.
- They play in tune.
- They don't hassle you.
- They have excellent instruments and play them well.

One bad thing about studio musicians:
- Sometimes they don't show up on time.

CONTRACTORS

Contractors are used as clearing houses for hiring musicians. Hiring a contractor eliminates the need for you to call each individual musician for your date. Contractors follow up, making sure everyone knows where the date is, what time it is, and what instruments (mutes, mallets, rentals, etc.) are needed for the recording. Contractors get paid double scale for their services and are worth every penny. They know who's best for what kind of music, as you will discover when you arrive at the session. Ask around for the names of good contractors when you need studio musicians.

Gibson Les Paul and friend.

ARRANGERS

Arrangers are used for a number of different reasons. You might hire an arranger to write string parts to rhythm tracks you've already recorded, or string and horn parts. You might hire an arranger to write an entire orchestration from your lead sheet. Or you might hire an arranger to fix what you've unwittingly messed up at great cost. An arranger is a member of the musician's union and will expect to conduct the sessions for which he's arranged music. It's good to work with him as early as possible in the project, because his input can be invaluable. He's had different experiences from yours and can introduce you to a broad perspective of sounds that could be useful to building your song. A good professional arranger will do his work in standard musical language and have parts copied out by a copyist (at extra cost) for the musicians to read at the recording session. He'll conduct the session, and make any necessary changes on the spot. While the arranger's fee is determined by the musician's union, some top arrangers will work only for over-scale payment. This is also true of some superstar musicians and engineers. In the case of some superstar musicians or engineers, they may even request a percentage of the artist's royalty on the record. They've got to be amazingly valuable to get this, but sometimes, in fact, they are.

Of course there are many recording sessions that are done without a formal producer, without studio musicians, contractors, arrangers, or assistant engineers. Sometimes all it takes is a self-contained band and an engineer to make a great record. Nobody worries about charts, overtime, or efficiency. It can take a whole day to get the right drum sound, three days to do a piano overdub, and six months to mix. While this type of situation is different from the "normal" studio situation, many of the same criteria of recording, mixing, and editing do apply. In the next sections, we'll examine the tools of the studio and how to use them to get the sound you want.

Functions of Basic Equipment

Neumann Solid State Condenser Microphones— left to right: U87, KM 86, KM 84

Neumann Solid State Condenser Microphone: U89 disassembled into its component parts.

MICROPHONES

Microphones can be discussed forever, because everyone has his own theories regarding their use . . . but for purposes of convenience, let's narrow the discussion down to two criteria: 1) the process by which the mike operates and 2) pickup pattern.

1. Processes

Condenser microphones require that an externally generated voltage be applied to them in order to operate. That is, they require battery or "phantom" powering from a separate power supply or from the mixing console. Because condenser mikes operate with electrically charged capacitors, you'd get no sound without the external powering. Generally speaking, a studio's "phantom" power supplies will serve condenser mikes requiring from 9-48 volts. Assuming that you're powered up, you have here a microphone widely regarded to have a better, smoother frequency response, a better response to transient peaks in signal, and a higher output to the mixing console. Condenser mikes are in every recording studio and are highly regarded for critical applications such as vocals, strings, and location recording. Some examples of excellent quality condenser mikes in-

clude the entire line of Neumann microphones, (U 89, U 87, U 67, U 47, KM 83, 84, 86) and the AKG models C-24, EB 414, and 452. Microphones by Schoeps and Sony are also well respected and widely used. Condenser mikes are not recommended for outdoor work or conditions where they'd be expected to undergo a lot of jostling.

Dynamic mikes are equally popular and are also used for many applications. They are less likely to overload and cause audible distortion than condenser mikes, require no external powering, and are more physically durable. (The Electro-Voice company hammers nails with them at their demonstrations.) In the studio, dynamics are very often used for miking drum kits, guitar amps, horn sections, and percussion instruments. This is not to say that they won't do equally well on vocals and strings, but many engineers gravitate toward the condensers for those applications. Dynamic mikes are also the standard of the PA (public address) setup, and are used in clubs, bars, and concert halls all over the map. Some examples of excellent dynamic mikes include Sennheiser models 421 and 441; Electro-Voice RE-20 and RE 15, and the ever-popular (and cheap) 635A; and from Shure, the SM 57.

Ribbon Mikes actually use a metal foil ribbon to transform acoustic energy (music) into electrical signal. These are the most delicate of the three types of mikes mentioned here, and are used considerably less often than either condensers or dynamics. Ribbon mikes are associated with a "warm" sound and are

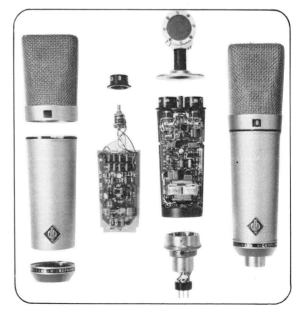

Clockwise from top left: Neuman Solid State Condenser Microphone: The Neumann U47 Cardiod microphone.

Sennheiser Dynamic microphone: MD 41.

Electro-Voice: Model RE20— Dynamic Cardioid microphone.

Electro-Voice Model 635A.

Electro-Voice Model RE15— Dynamic Cardioid microphone.

Sennheiser Dynamic microphone: MD 421

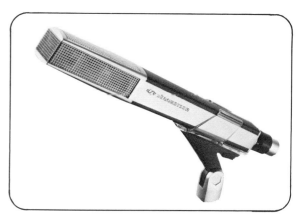
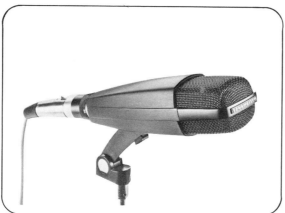

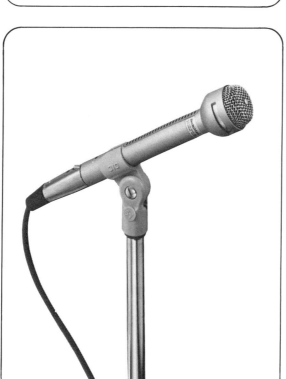
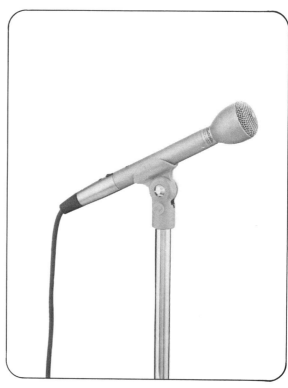

used for woodwinds and brasses. Beyer Dynamic makes a line of dynamic ribbon-microphones that combine the durability of dynamics with the operating principles of ribbons. Other popular ribbon mikes tend to look like survivors from the Golden Age of Radio, and frequently are. These are the RCA-44 and 77 types. If their ribbons are in good shape, they sound good, regardless of their age.

Shure:
SM57/65-3-D2

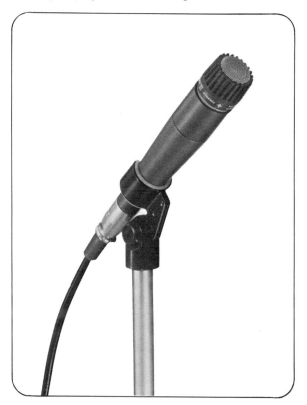

2. Pick-up Pattern

Pickup patterns determine the sensitivity of microphones to signals arriving from various places around the microphone's diaphragm. Polarity characteristics vary from model to model, but are categorized as being either **cardioid** (also known as uni-directional, with variations called **hypercardioid** and **supercardioid**), **omnidirectional** (also known as non-directional) and **bi-directional**.

Simply stated, a **cardioid** mike "hears" signals coming at it most accurately from the front, and tends to reject signals from the sides and rear. This is why it's called uni-directional. Cardioid mikes are by far the most popular mikes in studios, where some degree of isolation of instruments is required. By minimizing the "leakage" from other instruments in the studio, the cardioid pattern gives the engineer more control over the signal entering the microphone.

The **omnidirectional** mike is sensitive to signals coming at it from 360°, or all around. The omni is useful in the studio for recording background vocalists, where they can't all fit "in front of" a cardioid mike, or in miking a grand piano, where a cardioid might not pick up desired reflections of sound from the piano's lid. Omnis have the additional advantage of becoming cardioid at close range, while reducing a common cardioid problem, the "proximity effect."

The proximity effect causes a boost in very low frequencies when a cardioid mike is worked close to the source; this can result in a "boomy" sound, or in popped "p"s from a vocalist.

The last type to concern us is the **bi-directional** mike. As its name implies, it picks up equally from front and back. Conveniently, it also rejects unwanted sounds arriving from the sides of the mike. Bi-directional mikes are useful for a two-person interview, for recording two players facing each other, or for recording direct sound of an instrument blended with room sound. Bi-directional is not a very popular pattern, but it's good to have a couple around should the occasion arise.

High-quality condenser mikes will frequently have built-in switches that enable them to change their pickup patters from cardioid to omni to bi-directional, with graded stops in between. Other mikes have interchangeable capsules with various pickup patterns and frequency response characteristics. About the only other microphone feature that seems to be in general use is a bass roll-off switch. This switch engages a filter for low frequencies, reducing their volume at the output of the mike. The bass roll-off is used to compensate for the proximity effect, for excessive bass from the musician, or even to minimize the noise of an air-conditioning system in the room. The bass roll-off, like all other equalization and processing devices, should be used only when it's deemed necessary to achieve the desired sound. Otherwise, it colors the sound and contributes to a low-fidelity recording. Microphones may be labeled with a switch that says M or V or M_1, M_2, etc. These designations stand for *Music* and *Voice,* and indicate various stages of bass roll-off, as does this symbol:

CABLES

Cables are the wires that connect the mikes to the console, the tape recorders to the wall, your guitar to its amplifier. They are the most consistent trouble spots at the beginning of any recording session.

Most often studio cables have three conductors in them and are called "balanced." Audio signal, phantom powering, and noise are three things that commonly travel along these cables. The connectors at either end are called XLR's, male or female, and are three-pin connectors . . . one for each wire in the cable. Ends of the wires are soldered to these pins, which ultimately make a connection with a microphone on one end and the console on the other.

It's common for these connections to become unstuck during periods of heavy use, and the result can be a hum, buzz, loss of high-frequency response, loss of low-frequency response, or no signal at all. In addition, the shield of the cable (which acts as one of the three conductors) can become crushed and cause the same problems to occur. This happens when the Steinway gets rolled over the cables one time too many.

Input panel in studio: Mikes are connected to the console through this panel.

If you're having mike noise problems, or getting no sound at all, the mike cable is a good place to start looking for trouble. Replace it right away to see if the problem disappears. If it doesn't, perhaps the power supply wasn't turned on, the mike wasn't plugged in, or the engineer hit the wrong button. Don't panic.

The other cables that are important to you are called *phone* cables, and come in two basic types: three-conductor and two-conductor. The three-conductor cables are used in patch bays and for making stereo connections with one cable (like a headset cable). The two-conductor type, commonly known as "guitar cords," are used for interconnecting electric instruments to amps, fuzz boxes, wah-wah pedals, and the like. Two-conductor cables are "unbalanced" and are more susceptible to hums, buzzes, and RF (radio frequency) interferences than balanced cables. If you play an electric instrument, always bring at least one extra cable, preferably two or three, if you're using any foot-pedal devices. The engineer probably has a couple around, but there are never enough.

THE RECORDING CONSOLE

The console is the nerve center of any recording session. Rest assured that the engineer has looked at it, cajoled it, fixed it, kicked it, and caressed it until it feels as close to him as the family dog. The console accepts microphone signals at its inputs and routes them to tracks on the tape recorder through its outputs. Between those two stages are where some of the miracles and disasters happen.

On the input side of the console is a group of identical-looking faders. Above each fader is an equalizer, a trim pot or pads, buss assignments, echo and cue sends, panpots, pre/post switches, cut buttons, and a few other knobs, depending on the particular board. Each live microphone in the studio comes up on a different input module and is assigned (*buss assignment*) to a track on the tape recorder: Bass to Track 1, bass drum to Track 2, guitar to Track 12, etc. It's possible to combine several mikes on the same tape-track by using the same buss-assignment

number for each module. For example, if the drummer has eight tomtoms, you wouldn't want to assign them to eight different tracks, so tomtoms 1-4 might go to Track 20 and tomtoms 5-8 might go to Track 21. This way you've used up only two of your tracks.

Of course, once they're recorded together on the same track, you can't change the balance between any of the 1-4 or 5-8; you can only rebalance them one group vs. the other. This does not mean that it's better to use separate tracks, though. Theoretically, perhaps; but in practical terms, a good engineer can determine quite nicely what the relative balance in a drum set should be.

Having assigned the input (microphone) to a tape track, the engineer and producer will listen to the sound of that instrument. Auditioning each input prior to recording gives the engineer the opportunity to move mikes to more ideal placements, to change mikes, to determine correct level settings, and to decide whether equalization is required. Once this is determined, the engineer will send each microphone signal to the *cue mix* busses (the mono or stereo blend for the headphones) and to the *monitor echo* buss. These procedures allow each signal to appear in the musicians' headsets and at the input of the reverb chamber.

It's unusual to monitor a session with absolutely no reverb (echo), so each module takes advantage of its echo-send capability to enhance the sound. The echo that now appears in the control room speakers (and possibly in the headphones, too) does not go on the tape. It's only used for monitoring purposes, to make the sound more like the final product. Final decisions about echo and reverb are held off until the final mix takes place.

The *fader* is usually the bottom control in each vertical row of knobs and sliders. This, used in conjunction with trim pots, pads, and equalizers, is set to pass the optimum signal level along to the tape recorder. A separate control, either in the input module or elsewhere on the console, determines how loud the signal will be in the control room speakers (*monitor level*) and does not affect the level of the signal going to the tape recorder. So, if you're near the board and want to make something louder or softer, make sure you use the monitor pots, *not* the faders on the input section. The best way is to ask the engineer for more or less of the instrument in question.

The input section, just described, encompasses the largest part of the recording console. From this point on, consoles vary widely in shape and location of controls. Somewhere on the board is an *output* section. The outputs of the busses (*channel-send circuits*) are precisely calibrated before the session to make sure they're in perfect agreement with the inputs of the tape recorder, and they're the last step in the signal path before the music actually gets on tape.

There will be a *monitor* section, which is used for setting levels of individual channels for the control room speakers. There will be a *monitor-select* series of buttons that determine the source of the sounds

MC1 24 Track Recorder with Xedit two-inch editing block.

you hear in the control room. For example, they may be marked BUSS (output of the console), TAPE (playback from the master recorder), 2TR, 4TR, 8TR, PHONO, CUE, etc., and pressing the corresponding button lets you monitor the source of your choice.

Other controls on the console will include *master* level controls for CUE SEND, ECHO SEND, ECHO RETURN, TALKBACK, and a number of other buttons whose functions range from "soloing" a certain instrument or channel to muting the monitors while the engineer answers the phone. Newer consoles are likely to have a whole other complement of controls, with buttons marked READ, WRITE, NULL, and UPDATE. These refer to automated mixing, discussed in Chapter 11.

As you can see, the mixing desk, or recording console, is a complex routing and effects device, best left in the hands of the engineer. The particular criteria with which you must concern yourself are level, equalization, echo, and panning. You'll have a better grip on those concepts by the time you've finished this book or by the time you get to mixing your tape . . . whichever comes first.

THE MULTI-TRACK TAPE RECORDER

The multi-track machine has either 16, 24, or 32 tracks. It's a tape recorder somewhat similar in principle to the one you may have at home, but with important differences. Aside from differences in size and track capability, other important departures include construction, alignment capability, and cost. Multi-track machines are built better than home machines. With prices ranging from $20,000 to $100,000, you can assume that these machines will run at the proper speed, will have a lot less wow and flutter, and that the noise- and frequency-response characteristics are superior to any you've seen on a quarter-track home machine. These machines come that way from the factory and are kept that way through scrupulous maintenance.

MCI Auto Locator/ Remote Controller

Unlike home machines, professional recorders use a wide track-width, which results in a superior signal-to-noise ratio (or wider dynamic range before noise). All professional machines, from 2-track to 16-track, use this tape track-width. 24-track machines (or heads) use a smaller track-width, but generally employ outboard noise reduction devices such as Dolby or dbx to compensate for any loss in signal-to-noise ratio. Multi-track machines have precise calibration controls for each channel with respect to bias current, high- and low-frequency equalization, and levels for record and reproduce. In addition to these, a series of transport control pots is set so that the machine is always at the correct speed and tension. All these calibrations are performed by the maintenance crew at the studio, and are done in reference to a standard alignment tape and procedure. So, if the machines are properly calibrated, the only difference between the results of one tape recorder and another should be

the room in which you're listening and the speakers through which they're coming.

You can record on any track or combination of tracks at any time, depending upon which are selected by the engineer. Multi-track machines have a sync capability, whereby a pre-recorded signal (rhythm track, for instance) can be played back while the musician overdubs another part (vocal, guitar solo, etc.). When the composite is played back, everything is in perfect time (sync) with everything else. If there were no sync capability, your overdubs would appear a fraction of a second behind the rhythm tracks.

Most multi-track machines also have a variable-speed capability, which allows the engineer to slow down or speed up the tape. This is useful for recording an out-of-tune instrument to sound in tune, or increasing or decreasing the tempo of a song. Variable speed should be used sparingly though, for a couple of reasons. The timbral qualities of many instruments change drastically with wide variations, and the settings are hard to duplicate precisely.

Another popular feature for multi-track machines is a remote controller. This eliminates having to run over to the machine to turn it on, or stop it, or to punch in. Remote controllers frequently include buttons for making any or all of the tracks record-ready, for selecting tracks to play back in sync for overdubs, or for changing the source of the monitor signal from INPUT to TAPE. In addition, many of these controllers can be programmed to return to a pre-programmed position, indicated by a number on the display panel, which can represent the beginning of a song, the bridge, the kazoo solo, or whatever else you like. Some of them can remember several positions for future reference. Of course, these devices can control all the normal transport functions, like FAST-FORWARD, REWIND, PLAY, RECORD, and STOP.

THE TWO-TRACK MACHINE

The two-track machine is at least as important as the multi-track, for this machine will record the final mix to be sent out for transfer to master-lacquer disc. In theory, the two-track recorder is similar to a home machine in that it has only one pair of recording and playback channels, two sets of electronics, and uses ¼-inch tape. The two track machine will also be calibrated and aligned before every mixing session, and adjustments made with respect to azimuth, correct phase-relationship, level, bias, and equalization. Your recording is only as good as the two-track machine it's mixed on, so these machines must be in top form at all times. Standard high quality two-track machines include those made by Ampex (the ATR-100 is their newest and best), Scully, MCI, Telefunken, and Studer.

A final mix of the multi-track master is made to the two-track, and at this time, final decisions are made regarding balance, echo, panning, equalization, and special added effects. Some of these factors may be altered later, in what's called a "two-to-two" remixing situation, where the two-track master is remixed through the console to another two-track machine, or in mastering (disc cutting) where it's possible to change eq (equalization) limiting, or stereo perspective. In general, though, you should think of the original two-track mix as the last step in the process. Going two-to-two will cost you quality by adding another generation of tape hiss. Furthermore, making adjustments during disc mastering can be a monumental headache because the disc cutter's speakers never sound the same as the speakers at the mixing studio. You'll hardly ever be certain of what you're hearing unless you've worked in that mastering room several times before.

MONITORING EQUIPMENT

In order for you to hear what's going on in the control room, the inputs, outputs, tape deck, echo cham-

ber, and whatever other outboard gear you're using must ultimately be sent to a power amplifier and speakers. If you think of all that machinery as occupying the same space in the system as your pre-amp or receiver at home, you know that the next step is the power amp. It's the same in the studio. The last stage before the speakers, the studio power amp handles all the final output signals from the console. Studio power amps range from 150 to 600 watts per channel, depending on the speakers in the room and the thinking of the studio owner when he installed the system. There will be a basic two-channel amplifier for monitoring, an additional two-channel if you're mixing quadraphonic, probably a backup amp in case of failure of one of the others, and several smaller amps. Amps ranging from 40 to 300 watts per channel are used for driving headphones, studio playback speakers, alternate control-room speakers, and sometimes the talkback system. Some very popular and high-quality power amps used in studios include Crown, MacIntosh, Dyna, SAE, Phase Linear, and BGW.

The last step in the listening chain (except for the room itself) is the control-room speakers. Systems popular in studios today include Big Reds, Urei 813's, Altec 604's, Altec Model 19's, Westlake/Hidley systems, and JBL's of various designations. The debate over loudspeakers and monitoring is without doubt the most controversial area of audio discourse and we will not enter it here. For now, you want a speaker that will "translate" well to your home system and to the systems in the offices of record company executives. If your tape sounds great in the studio but lousy in Clive Davis's office, you can't tell Clive that he needs new speakers to listen to your stuff.

The idea of "translating" runs against the grain of the high-fidelity concept of listening. Most people buy speakers that will reproduce the music as accurately as possible, with minimal coloration. Of course, studios want good, clear-sounding speakers, but the overriding criterion is frequently not how good the music sounds, but how "standard" it sounds. Armed with the knowledge that tapes can be moved to different studios for overdubs and mixing, and that the product may be heard under a variety of less-than-ideal listening circumstances, studios frequently opt for a standardized type of sound. This is the reason for the overwhelming popularity of these few models of loudspeakers in studios. Most places will have a standard set of control-room monitors and at least one "accessory" pair of speakers, such as JBL 4311's or Auratone Sound Cubes. The accessory speakers permit the listener to judge what the music will sound like on a "home" or "car" stereo, respectively. In monitoring the final mix, it's always best to listen to the music on both sets of speakers. As to which set you ultimately use to mix, the producer almost always makes the decision based on his or her ears and experience. For what it's worth, I've recently been to all the A&R departments of three large record companies, and all the offices I visited were

Most studios are equipped with a grand piano.

equipped with JBL 4311's. This does not say that they're better than anything else, but they do seem to be in a lot of the right places.

Finally, the room in which you listen can have a profound effect on the sound because of reflective or absorptive surfaces in the room. As there is no standard room, complete accuracy is impossible, but two ways to approach it follow:
1) work in a control room that has been measured and corrected for inherent reverberation time and then acousti-voiced with 1/3-octave graphic equalizers, or 2) keep the speakers very close to you (called near-field monitoring) to eliminate the effects of the room itself.

As I've said, there is no ideal solution, but somehow the records manage to come out sounding good anyway. Experience, in the end, is still the best teacher.

STUDIO EQUIPMENT

Apart from the equipment in the control room just described, the studio itself, or recording room, has its own batch of goodies. Most studios maintain a stable of instruments, but you've got to know what's there before you start your session. Most portable instruments are expected to arrive with the musicians who play them, but studios routinely provide pianos, organs, some sort of drum kit, and an electric keyboard or two.

Drums come in all combinations in recording studios. Some studios supply a full set, and it's safe to assume that if a studio has a complete drum kit, it's a good one. Otherwise they'd have a lot of complaints. But it pays to check a kit out before sitting down to record. It could be that the heads need replacing or you need four tomtoms instead of two, or there aren't enough cymbal stands. Also, they are

Studio-drum kit— no extra charge.

usually tuned the way the engineer likes them—with blankets stuffed in the bass drum, and tape on the heads of the tomtoms. Drummers should re-tune as necessary, because no set stays in perfect tune for long. Most studios, though, supply just a bass drum, or a bass drum and set of tomtoms. If there ever were cymbals in the studio, they were probably stolen long ago. And, as most drummers prefer their own snares, cymbals and snare drums are almost always brought by the drummer.

Every studio will have a **piano** and probably a grand piano at that. These vary in quality as you might imagine, from horrible to excellent. The studio piano will be adequate for most pop, rock, jingle, and funk material, but may be only marginally suitable for jazz and probably unsuitable for classical. The most popular names are Steinway and Baldwin, with Yamaha gaining ground fast. A baby grand is not a grand and will never give the depth to be had from a grand; so if you need more than rhythm piano playing, look for a good-sized piano. Further, if a piano is more than slightly out of tune, you are in the wrong studio. Good studios have their pianos tuned at least once a week. Some are tuned once a day, and some are tuned before every session using piano. For classical piano recordings, a tuner is usually employed to stand by during the session and is expected to make sure that the instrument is always in perfect tune.

While the average studio piano is good enough for most things, jazz players will often shop around for a studio with a piano they like, and classical players will usually rent an instrument from the manufacturer. Pianos can also be rented from companies like Pro Piano (NY, SF, LA), which owns and rents different brands and styles suitable for any type of session or concert. Many studios have an old upright to be used just for "honky-tonk" effects. These are usually kept

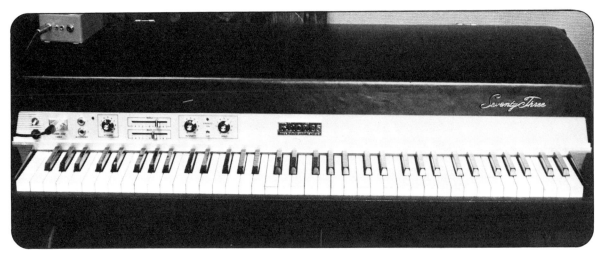

Fender Rhodes Electronic Keyboard—Model Seventy-Three

slightly out of tune to create the effect, but all keys should obviously be in working order.

Where the studio does not own, it will rent **electronic keyboards** for a session at the client's expense. Most sudios have an electric piano, either a Fender Rhodes or a Wurlitzer, which is sometimes supplied free. Beyond that, you're likely to find at least one small synthesizer and perhaps a Clavinet on hand, sometimes free, sometimes for an extra charge. Any special keyboards, such as a Prophet 5 or a Jupiter 8 synthesizer must be rented. The studio can do that for you if you don't own the one you need. A great many studios have organs on hand. Most commonly, you'll find a Hammond B-3 or M-3. These are usually free for the asking, as are the guitar and bass amps.

Guitar amps in studios are usually small compared to stage amps because the sound only has to reach a nearby microphone and perhaps a musician a couple of feet away. Fender amps are popular in New York studios, with the Twin Reverb running a strong lead. Other popular amps include the Fender Pro and Princeton models, the Mesa Boogie, Acoustic amps, and the Music Man line. Polytone amps, like the Mini-brute, are becoming increasingly popular in studios because of their light weight and exceptionally clean sound.

Bass amps are also a standard, with the Ampeg B-15 the most popular, followed by Acoustic. Again, these amps are most often used for feel rather than to create a gigantic sound, and serve very well. The studio will have from two to five guitar amps and one or two bass amps from which to choose. Beyond that, you can always rent the amp of your choice or bring one from home.

Amplifiers are famous for hums and buzzes that you never heard on the gig. Don't forget that the microphone hears the amp from very close, and magni-

"Tack Piano": Thumbtacks are placed on the hammers.

fies any inherent problems—from electronic noises to leakage from a wahwah pedal or phaser. In most cases, it's best to use the studio amps, because they're tried and true.

Direct Boxes are used to split the signal coming from an electric instrument into two signals. One of the two is fed through a transformer and over a mike cable into the console. The other is fed back out of

Hammond B-3 Organ: A studio standard.

Fender Twin Reverb and direct box: Common guitar recording technique.

the direct box into the instrument's amp. The direct box permits the engineer to get the instrument's signal right off the pickups of a guitar or bass, before the amp has a chance to color the sound, and it doesn't interfere with the sound going to the amp. Studios supply direct boxes.

The studio will also have a full complement of music stands (the sturdy, black variety) and stand lights, where necessary. If you decide to bring in a 60-piece brass band, they'll probably have to rent some extra ones and you may be required to pay for the rental.

It's a small point, but a recording studio is expected to be able to light any situation for recording, from mood lighting to full blast coverage, with adequate lamps for musicians who may be sitting in dark spots. Nothing is more of a drag than not being able to see the music in front of you or being stuck with 1000 watts of "on" or "off" when you're doing a lead vocal at two in the morning.

Basic Session Procedures

One of the biggest problems in a session of any size is knowing when to do what. The poor communication that can exist among participants in a recording can be astounding. This is due, at times, to a simple lack of experience; this chapter aims to substitute for some of the courses in "hard knocks" that you may otherwise have attended so that you can behave as a seasoned pro. Professionalism is the key. Generally speaking, the more "professional" your approach, the better the recording will be.

ARRIVAL AND SET UP

If a session is called for let's say 3 P.M., it's expected that all the musicians will at least be physically in the studio by that time. Depending on the type of session, they might also be expected to have their instruments out and ready to play. The assistant engineer will, by now, have set up all the chairs and music stands, set up and checked out all the microphones and headsets, and loaded the master recorder with tape and cued it to begin recording. He or she will have balanced the echo chambers, sharpened pencils, helped the rental people set up the drums, and will be at the ready for contingencies like the producer's showing up with an extra guitar player or a chorus of sixty.

The engineer will be at the console, greeting producer, arranger, and musicians, while keeping one ear open to the goings-on in the studio. He or she will be answering last-minute questions from the assistant or a musician, listening to extraneous noises from the console, the mike lines, the echo chambers. The engineer will, by now, know the exact instrumentation for the session, how many tracks are to be used for what, what the overdubs are planned to be, and if any special equipment is needed.

The producer has all the answers to the non-technical questions . . . most of the time. He knows which songs get recorded today, which musicians will show up at what time, approximately how many tracks will be needed, what equipment will be required, and who the guests and groupies are likely to be.

The arranger, if there is one, has prepared the charts, had the individual musicians' parts copied out, and planned for overdubs to complete the orchestration. He's in the studio, probably comparing notes with the musicians.

The contractor, again if there is one, has made sure that all the right musicians have been called and have arrived at the right studio with the right instruments. He has prepared union contracts covering their work for the session, and is there to chase down any latecomers, stragglers, or no-shows. During the session,

Typical studio setup for rhythm tracks. (Courtesy Sound Heights Studio— Brooklyn, N.Y.)

the contractor will let the producer know when a coffee break is due and generally run interference between the producer and the musicians as a group.

Clearly then, setting up a session to begin on time is a team effort. Considering all the technical factors, personnel, and information to be organized, it's a minor miracle when a session begins smoothly and on time. Nevertheless, most of the time they do because the participants are functioning as professionals.

TRACKS

The engineer and producer will decide together which instruments go on which tracks. There's a wide variety of possibilities, but in a common record album-type recording on a 24-channel tape, the track sheet usually looks like this for the basic session: (see page 32)

In the rhythm section recording, the mono instruments, including electric guitar and bass, will have at least one track each.

The piano, acoustic or electric, is sometimes given two tracks for a full stereo image. Most electric pianos have only one output and will get only one track on the tape; but the Fender Rhodes suitcase model has stereo outputs to take advantage of its built-in tremolo effect, and is often recorded on two tracks.

The drums can be recorded on anything from two tracks to eight, usually somewhere in between. The bass drum always gets its own track in pop, rock, disco, and jingles, and frequently in jazz as well. The snare drum frequently gets its own track, too, because it may need to be rebalanced with the rest of the kit later in the mix. The high hat (or sock cymbal) occasionally gets its own track, but strictly as a matter of preference among engineers; the exception to this is disco, where it always gets its own. The tomtoms and overhead cymbals are usually recorded on either two or three tracks. This creates a left-to-right perspective and some stereo interest when the drummer does a pass on the tomtoms or alternates beats on two overhead cymbals. The tomtoms and overhead cymbals, collectively called the "kit," can be recorded on two tracks by using the *pan pots* (like balance controls on a home amplifier) on each input module to create the left and right effect. They can also be recorded on three tracks, giving each of the three tomtoms its own track, and blending the cymbals into the stereo image.

The engineer will save lots of tracks for overdubs. If the rhythm section basics go smoothly, there may still be a horn section, strings, vocals, miscellaneous percussion, or sound effects to be added to the master tape, and these will require additional tracks. Plan for the maximum (leaving two for piano, for instance) and plan at least two completely empty tracks. You'll undoubtedly wind up needing them before the recording is finished. (see pg 33)

TAKES

A "take" in recording is much like a "take" in movie-making. Each recorded effort, whether a false start or a complete performance, is given a take number. The only substantive difference in logging (keeping notes of) takes is that in some studios, engineers prefer to use consecutive take numbers from the beginning of a session through to the end, so that the fourth song (for example) might begin with take 17 and end with take 22. Other studios (producers, engineers) will start at take 1 for each song or music cue to be recorded.

The purpose of noting and identifying these takes is for later recall for playback and overdubs. After a few false starts and possibly three good performances of a tune, it's easier to refer to "take 2" as the best performance than to indicate "the one where the bass played a B♭ harmonic in the fourth bar of the bridge." Engineers mark each take on a take sheet along with the title of the selection, and *slate* the take on the tape.

SLATES

This term, too, is derived from the movies, when the slate chalkboard was held in front of the camera at the beginning of a take to indicate scene and take number. Slate in recording is a verbal identification of the take number recorded a couple of seconds before the performance starts. The talkback button in the recording console has the provision for being connected to the master recorder, so that when the engineer says "Take 1" over the speakers and headphones, his or her voice goes on the tape at the same time. It's always good practice to *wait for the slate* before you begin playing. This ensures that you'll be able to find the correct take afterwards, during playback.

TALKBACK

The talkback system is used by the engineer and producer to communicate with the people in the studio. There are either one or two microphones attached to or built into the console, and these mikes are activated by pushing a button on the console marked TALK or TB. Depending upon where this circuit is wired, it will feed, in any combination, the studio speakers, the cue system, (headsets), the isolation booth, and the SLATE buss. Use of the talkback system will in most cases interrupt the signal going to the recorder and will always mute the control-room speakers to avoid feedback. In rare circumstances, should you need to address musicians while a take is in progress, be sure that the talkback is hooked up *only* to the cue circuit, and then make sure it won't

Take sheet

Date 1-6-81
Prod. J. Slick
Artist Trixie Flynn
Client Funkytown Rec.
Eng. E. McG. Reel # 2
Noise Reduc. Dolby
Other _____

TAKES

SELECTION	1	2	3	4	5	6	7	8
Melancholy Baby	FS	FS	LFS	C	FS	(C) TL		
Blue Bayou	(C) HTL	HTL						
Stardust	LFS	(C)	(INC) TL	Use 3 as insert to 2				
Air on a G String	C	(C)	FS	INC	C			
		(C) HTL	HTL					

Comments:
lunch tab $14.75

C = Complete
(C) = Choice Take
INC = Incomplete
FS = False Start
LFS = Long False Start
HL = Head Leadered
TL = Tail Leadered

Typical track sheet for basic tracks.

Client _Funkytown Rec._ Artist _Trixie Flynn_ Prod. _Johnny Slick_

Eng. _Fingers McGee_ Speed _15 IPS_ Noise Reduc. _Dolby_

Melancholy Baby

1	2	3	4	5	6	7	8
BS Direct	BD	SD	HH	OHL	OHR	EGTR	12 String

9	10	11	12	13	14	15	16
Acoustic Piano				Rhodes			Scratch Vocal

17	18	19	20	21	22	23	24

Blue Bayou

1	2	3	4	5	6	7	8

9	10	11	12	13	14	15	16

17	18	19	20	21	22	23	24

Finished track sheet before the mix.

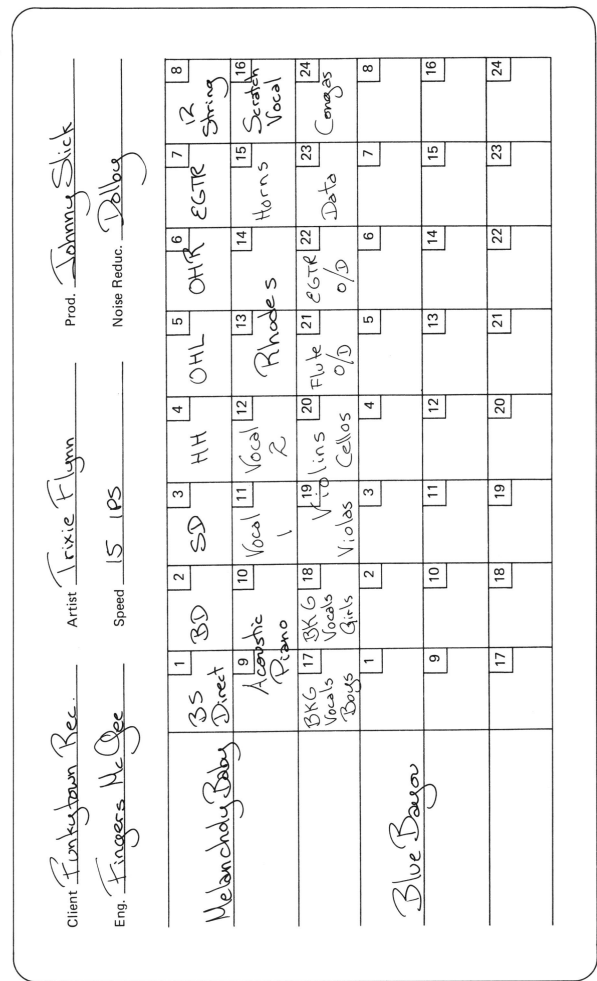

Client Funkytown Rec.

Eng. Fingers McGee

Artist Trixie Flynn

Speed 15 IPS

Prod. Johnny Slick

Noise Reduc. Dolby

	1 BS Direct	2 BD	3 SD	4 HH	5 OHL	6 OHR	7 EGTR	8 12 String
Melancholy Baby	9 Acoustic Piano	10 Vocal R	11 Vocal 1	12 Vocal R	13 Rhodes	14 Rhodes	15 Horns	16 Scratch Vocal
	17 BKG Vocals Boys	18 BKG Vocals Girls	19 Violins Violas	20 Violins Cellos	21 Flute O/D	22 EGTR O/D	23 Data	24 Congas
	1	2	3	4	5	6	7	8
Blue Bayou	9	10	11	12	13	14	15	16
	17	18	19	20	21	22	23	24

Isolation booth
for vocals,
acoustic guitar,
and drums.

put a click on the tape. This allows communication during performance but it is not widely used.

A common mistake is to lean close to the talkback mike when communicating from control room to studio. This is never necessary, because the talkback mike willpick up a voice anywhere in the vicinity of the console, and its level is set for a distant pickup. Speaking in a normal conversational voice while holding down the talkback button will get you through to the musicians without shattering anyone's eardrums.

ISOLATION OF INSTRUMENTS

There was a time when no one worried about isolation of instruments too much. Recording studios were more acoustically "live," and most things were recorded straight to mono with a few microphones. But with the development of multi-track, and the ability to punch in and redo certain parts, isolation became more and more a way of keeping options open in recording. Recording studios began to be built acoustically "dead." Sound-absorbent wall- and floor-coverings and surfaces in the studio minimized the reflections of sounds made by musical instruments, allowing virtually nothing but direct sound to appear at the microphone. In addition to creating deader rooms, studios expanded their use of sound baffles, called *gobos* (short for go-between), to further prevent the sounds of instruments from entering each others' microphones. And as a final touch, isolation booths became a popular part of studio life. In an isolation booth, an instrument could be considered to be almost totally free of leakage to or from the instruments playing outside the booth.

Now that the recording business had nearly complete isolation available, and, as a result, almost total

control over individual instrument signals, a problem arose: the music sounded sort of . . . well, dead. We had sacrificed natural acoustics for isolation and had just about thrown the baby out with the bath water. Fortunately, excellent reverberation devices were available to restore a kind of natural room sound, and they became more and more popular. In the 1970s, there was a tendency to backslide a little in the acoustics department, with some studios building rooms half-live/half-dead to accommodate both recording situations. It was now possible to record your rhythm section in the dead half of the room, then bring in the strings and horns and record them in the live half.

Another technique that became popular was moving from studio to studio. A project might begin in a small, dead room for rhythm and then move to another studio for overdubs. Studios went through endless experiments to satisfy their clients; to this day, some studios have motorized walls and ceilings that can be moved to expose one surface or the other. The ideal room remains one that doesn't feel dead to play music in—this makes musicians happy—while still being sufficiently sound absorbent to yield some isolation and control—this makes engineers happy.

There are many situations, though, where leakage and lack of separation are entirely desirable. Many jazz and classical records benefit enormously from being recorded in live, reverberant rooms, and some heavy rock groups sound better recorded live as well. The engineer can "take advantage of the leakage" to simulate the sound of a live performance, where the amps are up and the sound is bouncing all over the concert hall. In this kind of recording, there's a trade-off of isolation for musical spontaneity. But because that spontaneity is thought to be the "missing link" in overdub recording, most people consider the trade worthwhile if it doesn't get technically out of hand. There is that rare studio where one can achieve spontaneity with almost no leakage, too, but those are hard to find.

Total isolation is frequently desired for disco recording, since part of the disco sound is a "super-clean" recording. The producer and engineer may go so far as to record each instrument at a different time altogether, right down to the drum kit. It's not unusual to start out a disco track with just a bass drum, and then add snare drum, the high hat, then tomtoms and cymbals, piano, guitars, etc. Recording each instrument separately will yield an incredibly distinct sound because there's not even the remotest possibility of leakage; but recording this way takes up studio time and is very costly.

Meanwhile, back at the hypothetical recording session, the breakdown for purposes of isolation will run something like this: The drummer will either be in an enclosed booth or a "dead" corner of the room, facing out. In front of the drum kit there are likely to be three or four baffles, ranging in height from three to six feet. The taller ones have windows built into them so that the drummer can see and be seen. Electric guitars and basses will be seated in front of their respective amplifiers, and the amps will be enclosed on at least two sides by short (3-4 feet high) gobos. The acoustic piano will be draped with moving blankets, and the lead vocalist or acoustic guitar, or both, will be in isolation booths. Electric keyboard outputs will be fed direct to the console with their amps either off or turned down. Lines of sight will be maintained so that everyone sees everyone else, and the conductor, if there is one, will be at some central place with a small communications mike.

HEADPHONE BALANCES

Right at the beginning of the session, the engineer will either put on a headset or punch the CUE button on the monitor panel and try to get a good balance for the headsets. Musicians will then be asked if the headset mix or "cans" are OK. Someone may request that his or her instrument be more prominent in the cue mix. If there is only one cue system (circuit), all the musicians will hear the same mix, and that person's instrument will be louder for everyone. Possible solutions: 1) use separate cue mixes, if the console has that capacity (this takes additional time); 2) put one ear of your headset behind your ear, so you can hear your own instrument "live" while you hear the others through the remaining headset; or 3) go back to the original mix and live with it.

Asking for stereo cue or echo in your headset should be reserved for sessions in which time is not a factor. (Some boards are not equipped for either, in which case you're out of luck.) Even if they can be provided, they represent an additional time investment. There is no question that you need to hear a clearly defined bass, enough drums so that you can feel the beat comfortably, enough keyboard so you can hear the chords, and whatever else is necessary for you to do the best job you can. But the cue system was not designed to be a sensuous listening experience. What you want to hear is what you need to hear.

The engineer will always try to give you a cue mix that's comfortable to listen to and has enough instruments to get you where you're going. You can re-

quest anything you like, of course, from echo to strings and horns to more of yourself. When recording with other musicians on a mono cue, remember that any changes in the balance will affect their headsets as well as your own, so try to achieve a sound that's effective for everyone.

CLICK TRACK

When recording a commercial jingle or a film score, or any music that goes along with visual images, producers use what is called a "click" track. This is a digital metronome whose sound appears in your headsets as a loud click. The digital metronome is calibrated to correspond to frames-per-second on film, and is used by the composer or arranger to determine exactly the tempo and length of the music cue (selection). The click is played through the headsets and frequently printed on the tape as well, on its own track. Click can also be used in making records, to maintain a rock-steady pulse (although many musicians hate to use it because they feel it makes the performance too rigid). Engineers will usually shut off the click in the headsets between takes, but they can be reminded to do so if they forget.

PAPERWORK

If you're in the studio recording a demo or an album with a self-contained group, there's not much paperwork to worry about. But any session where union musicians are involved requires a union contract and W-4 forms. In order to file a union contract for a record date, someone concerned must be a signatory to the American Federation of Musicians Recording Agreement. This person is responsible to the union for seeing that all the musicians are paid the prevailing scales, plus health and welfare benefits and pension fund contributions. Each musician on the date supplies the producer (or contractor) with a W-4 form containing his or her name, address, number of dependents, instrument, union local number, membership number, and social security number. Some musicians have pre-printed W-4's but those who don't

W-4 Form

A.F. of M. Phono-
graph Recording
Contract

Please type or print with ball point pen on hard writing surface and press firmly. Make sure all copies are legible.

(Employer's name) _____

Phonograph Recording Contract

AMERICAN FEDERATION OF MUSICIANS

This Page to Pension Fund

≦ 447694

Local Union No._____

OF THE UNITED STATES AND CANADA

THIS CONTRACT for the personal services of musicians, made this _____ day of _____, 19_____, between the undersigned employer (hereinafter called the "employer") and _____ musicians (hereinafter called "employees").   (including the leader)

WITNESSETH, That the employer hires the employees as musicians severally on the terms and conditions below, **and as further specified on reverse side.** The leader represents that the employees already designated have agreed to be bound by said terms and conditions. Each employee yet to be chosen shall be so bound by said terms and conditions upon agreeing to accept his employment. Each employee may enforce this agreement. The employees severally agree to render collectively to the employer services as musicians in the orchestra under the leadership of

_____ as follows:

Name and Address of Studio _____

Date(s) and Hours of Employment _____

Type of Engagement: **Recording for phonograph records only.**   Plus pension contributions as specified on reverse side hereof.

WAGE AGREED UPON $_____
                                                              (Terms and amount)

This wage includes expenses agreed to be reimbursed by the employer in accordance with the attached schedule, or a schedule to be furnished the employer on or before the date of engagement.

To be paid _____
                                      (specify when payments are to be made)

Upon request by the American Federation of Musicians of the United States and Canada (herein called the "Federation") or the local in whose jurisdiction the employees shall perform hereunder, the employer either shall make advance payment hereunder or shall post an appropriate bond.

Employer's name and _____ (Name of Record Company)	Leader's name _____	Local No._____
Authorized signature _____	Leader's signature _____	
Street address _____	Street address _____	Phone No._____
City State Phone	City	State

Name of Artist or Group_____

(1) Label Name_____   Session No._____

Master No.	No. of Minutes	TITLES OF TUNES	Master No.	No. of Minutes	TITLES OF TUNES

(2) LOCAL UNION NO.	(3) LOCAL UNION CARD NO.	(4) EMPLOYEE'S NAME (Last, First, Initial) HOME ADDRESS (Street, City, State & Zip)	(5) SOCIAL SECURITY NUMBER / (6) MARITAL STATUS & EXEMPTIONS	(7) DOUBLING	(8) TOTAL SCALE WAGES	(9) CARTAGE	(10) 10% AFM-EPW	(11) H & W

FOR FUND USE ONLY:

(12) Total Pension Contributions (Sum of Column (10)) $_____
Make check payable in this amount to "AFM & EPW Fund."
(13) Total Health and Welfare   (Sum of Column (11)) $_____

Date pay't rec'd_____Amt. paid_____Date posted_____By_____

AFTRA Recording Contract

Phonograph Record Sessions Report _____   Schedule A & B
and P & W Report   Company Name

                                               Address   Job Number

                        P&W Account No:_____

American Federation of Television and Radio Artists
    1350 Avenue of the Americas   1717 No. Highland Avenue
    New York, NY 10019   Hollywood, CA 90028   It is the responsibility of the Member to file a pink
    Tel - (212) 265- 7700   Tel - (213) 461 - 8111   copy of the report with the AFTRA Local Office
    1012 17th Avenue South   307 N. Michigan Avenue   within 48 hours of the session and deliver all other
    Nashville, TN 37212   Chicago. IL 60601   copies to employer at end of session.
    Tel - (615) 256 - 0155   Tel - (312) 372 - 8081

Type of Recording	Single	Album	Classical	Other

Date of Employment	Recording Studio	Address

Featured Artist	Label

Producer	Address	Phone No.

Song No.	Record (Title)	Over Dub	Playing Time*	Song No.	Record (Title)	Over Dub	Playing Time*
1				5			
2				6			
3				7			
4				8			

* Give playing time only if over 3½ minutes on any side.

Featured AFTRA Artist

Social Security Number	Name Last	First	Middle Initial	Song No.	Time From	To	No. of Sides	No. of Hours	Gross Compensation

Other Performers

Social Security Number	Name Last	First	Middle Initial	Song No.	Category	Time From	To	No. of Sides	No. of Hours

This Engagement governed by and subject to the
applicable terms of the AFTRA National code of   Total All Gross Compensation _____
Fair Practice for Phonograph Recordings_____   _____ 7 3/4% AFTRA Pension & Welfare Contribution _____
                                    Company Name

Key To Category
Soloists - Duos	S	Groups 17 - 24	S17	Narrator	N
Groups 3 - 8	S 3	Groups 25 Plus	S25	Sound Effects	SE
Groups 9 - 16	S 9	Contractor	C	Step - Out	SO

Additional Remarks

Signature of Employer or Representative	Signature of AFTRA Member	Phone No.	Date

RD 1645 5/75 _____

TO PENSION & WELFARE OFFICE WITH CHECK

will fill out blanks given to them by the contractor or engineer. (Most studios keep a supply on hand.) The producer then turns the W-4's over to a secretary or to the contractor, who makes up the union contract and hands it in to the union along with the musicians' checks and the other contributions to union funds. Frequently, musicians pick up their checks a few weeks later at the union office. In some cases, checks can be mailed directly to the musicians or handed out at the session, but the union contract still has to be handed in.

It is possible to do (and sponsor) a recording session without being a signatory to the AF of M agreement . . . no filling out of forms or anything. But this is in violation of union rules and can place the musician in a bad position. Many musicians will not work unless the situation is handled "by the Book." Everyone has a limited budget, no matter what the project is; but it's always best to play by the rules. In the end, it keeps everyone happier, and you don't lose friends through misunderstandings.

Similar contracts must be filed for recording film, jingles, and TV. Vocalists belong to a different union, the American Federation of Television and Radio Artists (AFTRA), which has a whole other set of contracts and rules. As the paperwork gets thicker, it becomes apparent that a contractor is a good idea for a recording project involving more than just a few people.

WORK ORDERS AND RENTALS

The office at the studio will probaly have filled out a work order for your session, specifying names of producer, artist, and engineer, number of hours booked, other services required (such as editing, mixing, tape copies, etc.) and the producer may be asked to sign the work order following the session, to verify and authorize the time and services used. If you've asked the studio to rent a musical instrument or special piece of outboard equipment for your session, there will be an invoice floating around for that, too.

Ultimately, the producer and/or the record company will receive invoices from the studio or studios used, the rental companies (outboards, drums, electric piano), freelance engineer if used, musician contractors, photographers, hotels, limousine services, and anyone who has supplied services for a recording project.

A FEW WORDS ABOUT STUDIO TIME

Almost every studio around works within the following guidelines, and it pays to know them. To begin, the client is responsible for time booked; i.e., if you book from noon to six P.M. and finish the record at 4 P.M., you've still got to pay the other two hours. Most studios will offer a "bumper" of one hour. If you plan to record for six hours, but want a seventh (bumper) hour available that you won't be charged for if you don't use it, book "six plus one" when calling in your session. If you're booked at 12 noon, but the bass player doesn't show up until 1:30, you're still responsible for the time from noon on. The clock starts at the time booked, assuming the studio is ready, not when you start recording. Finally, cancellation of time without penalty usually requires at least 48 hours' advance notice. Read the studio's rate card carefully or ask about the conditions of hire before you commit to studio time.

Recording the Basic Tracks

The expression "basic tracks" refers to the original recording of a multi-session project in which the rhythm section plays its parts prior to the recording of any solos, vocals, or string and horn parts (sometimes called "sweetening"). Basic tracks, then, usually consist of drums, piano, bass, and guitar. (For the purposes of this section, we're talking about music other than classical and jazz, for which basic tracks are not done.)

Because they're the first to be recorded, basic tracks are principally concerned with several factors. Tempo, key, and "feel" are the most obvious, because after the basics are recorded, it's too late to change any of those. The overall form of the song has been agreed upon, and the artist's key has been established. At this point in a project, the producer and artist may work together with the rhythm section to attain the precise sound they need for the song. The relatively small number of musicians present and relaxed atmosphere provides the producer with the opportunity to experiment in ways that may not have been possible up until this point, and certainly will not be possible later.

The artist, too, will be available to sing a guide, or "scratch" vocal. This vocal, sung while the rhythm section is being recorded, gives the musicians the support of the melody and lyrics while they play. Occasionally these scratch vocals turn out to be excellent performances and they're kept and issued as final vocals; but most often, the artist will redo his or her part at a later time.

Since few musicians are involved, the basic tracks give the engineer the opportunity to get the sound of the song recorded as cleanly as possible. Each instrument is listened to critically for sonic criteria, and every effort is made to get as close as possible to a great sound from the start. Although there are only a few musicians, isolation is a big factor here. Wherever possible, the engineer will seek to reduce any leakage between instruments. All the musicians will wear headsets to hear each other and the producer from the booth (control room). With this isolation, if a single part needs to be changed later, it can be done without ruining the other tracks. In the most isolated situations, in fact, an entire bass or piano part might be redone without the listener's ever noticing.

AMPS VS. DIRECT

There is almost always some controversy as to whether a guitar or electric bass should be miked at the amp or taken direct to the board. Once again, direct would lead to total isolation, but would miss the sound created by the amp/speaker combination. Most studios are able to accommodate a player who wants his amp on and still be able to achieve minimal leakage, assuming the amp isn't on very loud. Some studios just can't get that kind of separation, though, so it becomes a choice of one or the other. At this point, the producer has to weigh the need for isolation against the quality of sound coming from the instrument and the feelings of the musician in question. It's true that a guitar taken direct may be fed back out into the studio and through a guitar amp during a subsequent session, or as late as the mixing session, and will create the sound that was desired in the first place; but this takes additional time and won't placate an unhappy guitarist.

As to the electric bass, it almost always sounds better with just a direct feed . . . no amp, except in rock and roll, where the preference seems to be for the amp sound. Acoustic bass with a pickup will sound good direct, but will be enhanced by the use of a mike on the instrument. Direct-only pickups of acoustic bass can be successful, except when the bass is being bowed. I've found only one pickup that I think sounds good bowed, and that's the Polytone. Most of the others, including the Shadow, Underwood, and Barcus Berry sound find with pizzicato bass; but because they're mounted directly on the bridge of the instrument, they sound thin with a bow. Getting back to the electric bass, it's also common practice, when taking the bass direct, to have the player turn up his volume and treble controls all the way. This presents the best and most consistent signal to the recording console, and this signal is easily equalized or limited as necessary. For purposes of recording, the Fender Precision bass is most popular and gives a characteristic sound, where other instruments will take more work and time to achieve that sound. Techniques for making the bass notes clearer and better articulated include playing with a flat pick and/or playing near the bridge of the instrument.

HOW TO GET "THAT" DRUM SOUND

"That" drum sound is a particular combination of sounds that I'd heard on records for years before I was able to achieve it. It began for me on Carly Simon's "No Secrets" album, and continued with Paul Simon's "Still Crazy . . . ", Janis Ian's records, and on into Barry Manilow's and many others. It involved a combination of tuning, echo, and drum size. After seven years as a professional recording engineer I was finally able to achieve what I'd been hearing all that time. After reading about it, you may think it's not "the" sound you were looking for, or you may get it in a different way, but this is what works for me: The snare drum should be a big one if you want a big sound. The snares should be of moderate tension and the top head tuned a little on the loose side, but not sloppy loose. The bass drum should have only the batter head on it, and should be stuffed with a heavy density pillow or small blanket, weighted down with the bottom of a mike stand or a good sized brick. The degree to which the padding is pushed up against the front head will play a big part in determining the sound of the drum, as will the position of the microphone. What I look for in a bass drum is a sharp attack with a good bottom (low-frequency response) and absolutely minimim decay time. In other words, the sound of the drum should die away almost immediately. The final word on bass drum recording, if your music relies heavily on that drum, is to try using a wooden beater for extra tight attacks.

The tomtoms are the key component to my ideal drum sound. They should be made to produce a sound that glisses from one pitch to another, similar to the sound of the Syndrum, but not so high or electronic sounding. This sound can be achieved by starting out with hydraulic heads . . . the kind made from two layers of plastic with oil between them. They seem to sound best in the studio situation. Leave the bottom head on the drum to get the best tone, and most important, tune the heads perfectly. Tuning drum heads means more than just turning screws at random until the sound is close to what you thought you wanted. By placing one finger in the center of the head with a little pressure and tapping lightly with a drumstick at a point on the head near each tuning screw, you can hear the differences in pitch between the screws. Tune them all to the same pitch. Then if the drum sounds too high or too low, tune the whole drum up or down by turning the screws the same amount all around the drum. Recheck by placing a finger in the middle and tapping each point again. You should have a tomtom that sounds full, in tune, and "groans" a little bit when you hit it. Three or four of these, tuned to relative pitches, will produce a fill or pass that's satisfying. I've always thought that a lot of recordings included a tomtom sound that was like larger or smaller garbage cans, and that sound has ruined a lot of records for me. I hope this solution is of some help.

Rounding out the kit is the high hat and cymbals. I've found that thinner high hat cymbals work better, especially in disco, because they sound light and have an inherently better high-frequency component. The air noise created by the suction of the two high hat cymbals can be avoided in two ways: 1) drill a couple of holes in the bottom cymbal to let the air escape, or

2) bend out (warp) the edge of the bottom cymbal. Air noise can be a problem when the high hat is close-miked with a condenser mike, as it commonly is. As to the overhead cymbals, each drummer usually has a preferred set, and with very few exceptions that works out just fine. Most good cymbals will record quite well. Where possible, try to avoid the Chinese-type cymbal with the little flat cup in the middle and sizzle cymbals with metal rods attached to them.

There are many approaches to microphone technique for the drums. Most commonly, everything in the kit gets its own mike, except for the overhead cymbals, which are usually covered with a stereo pair of mikes. These overhead mikes pick up and localize the cymbals in the stereo spectrum and add a distant perspective to the overall drum sound that can be useful. Other techniques include miking the snare drum from under and over the drum, mixing the sounds to get the desired effect, using one mike to cover both snare drum and high hat, and using one mike for each pair of tomtoms.

Which mikes are used is strictly a matter of preference. Each engineer has developed a selection through his or her own experience. My personal preferences run to Sennheiser MD 421's for the toms, Electro-Voice RE-20 for snare and bass drum, and AKG 452 condensers for high hat and overheads. I've used other mikes that were equally suitable, including the Neumann U-87 and U-67 for tomtoms, the Shure SM-57 for snare drum, and the Electro-Voice 666 for bass drum (no longer on the market); but I subscribe to the theory that there are almost no "bad" mikes . . . just bad technique. I generally place my mikes in cardioid pattern and as close to the drum as possible without touching. This allows for some separation between the drums. Sometimes the bass roll-off switch is employed to compensate for the proximity effect of using cardioid patterns at such close range.

THE ELUSIVE GRAND PIANO

The grand piano is at once the easiest and most difficult of instruments to record. Any mike just about anywhere in the piano will get the sound down with no trouble at all, but it seems every time I record a piano, a different sound is called for, depending on the music. At times, the music needs a certain percussive quality, where the attack of the piano is almost as important as the notes it plays. At other times, it's got to sound ethereal and distant, even in a pop context. In a simple rhythm-section recording, the piano can often be miked with one microphone. The best compromise position I've found for this type of recording is to place the mike over the second tone hole in the sound board (looking from the keyboard side). This position seems to cover all the notes and minimizes noise from hammers and dampers.

More frequently, however, stereo piano is called for, and each microphone signal is sent to a separate

Draping a grand piano for isolation.

channel on the tape. There are many ways to approach this. A pair of crossed cardioids placed center and about three feet above the strings is one way to do it. A spaced pair, one at the front over the high strings and another at the bottom over the low strings is another way. These two techniques will yield a good, basic sound and a good stereo spread, but don't do much for the attack or percussive effect. The best percussive effect is achieved by placing a mike at each end of the keyboard, just behind the tuning pins and over the strings. This technique takes account of the hammers hitting the strings and rejects the reverberations introduced by reflections off the lid of the piano. Other possibilities in recording a

piano for basic tracks include a contact pickup made by Helpinstill or Countryman, to name two.

Taking the lid off the piano altogether, building the piano into a little booth, recording it with the full stick up (concert position) and a lot of moving blankets, or half stick (recital position) again with blankets are among several approaches used in piano recording. It's difficult to isolate an acoustic piano from the rest of the room, especially the drums, so be prepared. If all else fails, you can lay down a guide track with the electric piano taken direct to the board and overdub the acoustic piano later on. This is only necessary where leakage is a big factor, though. Most of the time, a little leakage is fine and need not be

*A possible drum-
miking setup.*

worried about. Electric pianos, as mentioned, can always be taken direct. The most popular electrics are Fender Rhodes and Wurlitzer models.

CLASSICAL RECORDING

To spend a moment in the classical department, it should be noted that the acoustic quality of a concert hall is fondly regarded in classical circles. This means miking the piano from a distance of 12 or 15 feet and up to 10 feet in the air. This will not be possible in your average dead-sounding studio, because the instrument will just sound "off-mike." When recording classical piano, or classical anything for that matter, it's best to have a nice, big, reverberant room in which to work. If you can't find a recording studio with live enough sound, you've got to go on location. Your local studio engineer will probably know a colleague who specializes in that type of recording, if he doesn't do it himself.

5 | Live Recording in the Studio

"Live" is the term applied to a recording situation in which all the musicians play at the same time, similar to a live situation on stage. There was a time when all recording was done "live." Early recording technology dictated that everyone play at once while the results were transcribed onto a wax disc, or later on, a mono or two-channel stereo tape. It wasn't until the 1950's that overdubbing became available to studios, though the innovations of the guitarist/inventor Les Paul and his collaboration with the Ampex corporation. While live recording is antithetical to disco and *most* current popular recording, most rock and roll, jazz, and classical performers still record this way. This is not because they are necessarily old fashioned, but because some types of music making are wholly dependent upon communication between the musicians. And since jazz, classical, and rock and roll musicians tend to at least acknowledge their debt to earlier artists and forms, the "live" technique has survived, at least to some degree.

ROCK AND ROLL

When I speak of rock and roll, I hope you understand that I'm talking about everything from Buddy Holly all the way to The Cars. Whatever the differences inherent in these two acts, they share the hard-edged feel of a spontaneous "group" sound that partially defines the term "rock and roll." Soft-rock, folk-rock, soul, electronic music, fusion and other types of music may share certain features of rock and roll, but not the driving need to make the sound with everyone playing together.

Rock and roll bands can be anything from a simple guitar-bass-drums trio to two guitars, bass, drums, keyboard, horns, background and lead vocals. They are usually self-contained units and not made up of studio musicians. As self-contained units which have performed, we assume, on stage a great deal, they have very definite ideas about the group sound, and what each member needs in order to do the job properly. Amongs these ideas is the feeling that the musicians should be able to play at a sound-pressure level (volume) that is beyond what would be acceptable under "normal" studio conditions. Although the producer and engineer may be able to convince the band that they don't need to play through a six-foot-high stack of amplifiers, it's likely that they'll insist on at least a small stack. Because the sound of a real rock band is partly created by the volume and proximity of the musicians and amplifiers, this attitude is justifiable to an extent, even considering the limitations of a recording studio's size. There will be inevitable leakage from amps to drums, from drums to acoustic piano, and so on. But since it's unlikely that a particular part will have to be overdubbed later, the need for isolation is not as critical as in the other kinds of recording. It's more likely that the band would record an additional take of a song if someone messes up, rather than contemplating an overdub. The leakage will actually contribute to the band's live sound, providing it's not out of control.

The degree to which the leakage can be managed depends on the particular studio you're working in, and in this situation, you're in the best shape with a very absorptive room. It needn't be totally dead, but you want to avoid a lot of reflections and natural room reverberations. Lines of sight should be scrupulously maintained because everyone needs to see everyone else for the purposes of making and taking cues for rhythmic figures, solos, and endings. If it's a loud session, it's unlikely that the cue system will provide the musicians with exactly the sound they want if for no other reason than that they won't get the feel of the band in a headset. The best approach is to suggest that the musicians wear one ear of the headset and have one off. This allows them to hear their own instruments and those nearby "live," and use the earphone for harder-to-hear things like the bass drum, keyboard, or electric bass.

Care should be taken to use highly directional microphones. Mikes with broad pickup patterns will create an off-axis leakage that may render the sound unpleasant. The thing to remember is that leakage in itself isn't inherently bad—in fact it can be an important factor in making a good rock and roll sound—but the *type* of leakage you're getting is the critical difference, as it can range from complementary, when the tape sounds like a recorded concert, to disastrous. Off-axis response, phase cancellations, and distorted amps can make it sound as if it were recorded in an airplane hangar with a telephone mike!

JAZZ RECORDING

Jazz recording is my particular specialty. Over the years, I've produced and/or recorded well over 350 jazz albums under a variety of conditions, from live in a concert hall straight to a 2-track recorder, to over-dubbing a single saxophone player in a 24-track studio situation. By and large, jazz musicians and producers couldn't care less if you used a 2-track or a 24-track recorder, as long as they can all play together.

Since jazz is an improvisatory art, it's imperative that the musicians be able to interact. They need to hear and see each other clearly to pick up on each other's ideas, riffs, licks, and moods. What makes good jazz great is the way the players create off each other. This is why most jazz is recorded live. The use of amplifiers is restricted to guitar players and the occasional bass player. The amps are usually not on loud at all, but just enough to provide a little more support for the musicians.

Older jazz players would still prefer to avoid the use of headsets, booths, and too many mikes whenever possible; they look to simulate the atmosphere of a club or concert when they record. Although they're generally willing to make concessions to the headsets and mikes, they will hardly ever agree to overdub a part for purely sonic considerations. I've been in many situations where the tenor sax player insisted on standing right next to the drummer to get his "feel." Of course, this is far from desirable for controlling the saxophone sound, but choosing a room and engineer that will permit a certain amount of flexibility can be invaluable for jazz dates. When you remember that happy musicians play better, you do what you can to keep them happy, within the limits of good recording.

In a typical mainstream-jazz studio situation, you might have a saxophone, a trumpet, acoustic piano, acoustic bass with a pickup, and a set of drums. It's best to set up in an intimate way so that no one has to holler around corners or over mikes to communicate with the other musicians. You won't be dealing with excessive volume levels here, so that's one area where you can breathe easy. Stereo miking of the piano, mixing the bass pickup with a mike, and stereo miking the drums with as few as four microphones will yield the "true" sound of the rhythm section fairly well.

Jazz drummers almost always bring their own drums. You may find their sound unusual, but that is "their" sound and, as such, is part of the music they create. You'll find most of them prefer to have both heads on the bass drum. The toms are tuned a little higher than you might like them, and there may be a favorite cymbal that sounds odd to your ears; but in jazz, the drummer's been hired partly because of the way his drums sound. In getting a set of jazz drums ready to record, you might suggest that a wallet be put on the snare drum to reduce the ringing, or ask him if thinner cymbals are available for the high hat, but jazz drummers don't want you to be re-tuning their tomtoms or taking heads off anything.

Horns in a jazz date are miked and recorded the same as in any other date. The only differences here are that, in the course of a solo, a jazz player may wander off mike a bit (. . . certainly more than would a horn player on a pop date). Choosing and positioning a mike with a generous pickup pattern are to the recording's advantage. You may also find that jazz players are given to a wide dynamic range, from pianissimo to fortissimo during solo passages. In section work, one can pretty much set levels and not worry about them too much, but jazz may call for some judicious limiting on occasion, to compensate for bursts of dynamic energy. The acoustic piano in jazz (at least in mainstream, bebop and traditional jazz) is best recorded sounding as "real" as possible. The mikes-over-the-hammers technique will work, but it's not the most desirable sound. Try to use a stereo pickup that accounts for the natural reflections inside the piano.

The acoustic bass will sound best with a microphone only, but the bass player's proximity to the drummer usually makes it necessary to use a combination of direct pickup and microphone. Again, bowing can sound very false with most pickups, so I suggest the Polytone.

CLASSICAL RECORDING

Although this promised to be a discussion of live recording in the studio, the plain fact is that most classical music isn't recorded in the studio. Most classical music is recorded on location, in large halls. But we'll deal with that in a moment.

There are certain types of classical (or "art," or "concert") music that can be successfully recorded in studios. Much twentieth-century music (or "modern" music, as it's sometimes called), for example, is better served by the dry, non-reverberant acoustics of the recording studio. Thus it's not unusual to book studio time to record a string quartet by someone like Elliott Carter. In these situations, multi-miking and multi-tracking are common. Use of baffles, gobos, and headsets is very limited in classical recording in general, but in this case the dry sound would serve well. Typically, the recording is done much like a pop recording, with one mike per instrument and one instrument per channel. The channels are remixed at a later date.

Some, although very few, recording studios are big enough and live enough sounding to record the balance of the classical literature. Out of about 150 recording studios in New York, for example, there are perhaps six where you get an acceptable sound for classical music. (These are, in my opinion, Media Sound, A&R Recording, Columbia, Vanguard, National Recording, and RCA Studios.) And even then, not every room is right for every piece of music. Generally speaking, classical music is best served by on-location recording.

Location or live recording of art music is, for a couple of "classical" reasons, subject to more controversy than any other type. Classical music listeners have among them a disproportionate number of people who call themselves "audiophiles." These are people who maintain very expensive stereo systems at home, who spend endless hours reading about the latest megabuck phono cartridge, and who like their recordings as pure as possible. There's nothing wrong with any of this, but many audiophiles tend to go overboard in the pursuit of technical excellence—to the extent that the term "splitting hairs" becomes an understatement.

Most listeners believe that a classical recording should sound like a live performance in a concert hall. Toward that end, there's a great fondness for reproducing the "ideal" listening position in a recording. This often involves recording with a single stereo microphone, or two monaural microphones placed at a healthy distance from the orchestra or chamber group. The theory is that if the listener were sitting in the hall with the orchestra, this is how his ears (two transducers, microphones) would hear the music. I've found that this method of recording yields highly satisfactory results in almost all classical situations. The key component here is the hall in which the music is to be recorded. This type of recording can't be done in a typical recording studio because of the acoustics of the studio. When instruments are played in a good hall, the reverberations begin within milliseconds of the original sound and continue to reflect off the walls, ceilings, and furniture at a steadily decreasing rate of volume for from about 2 to 8 seconds, depending on the hall. This factor is called the "decay time" of the reverberation. Studios are built to have relatively short decay times and minimal reflections of the original sound. Remember in the studio we try to eliminate leakage from one instrument to another. In a concert hall, leakage is a tremendous part of the sound, and in fact, is what makes one hall sound different from another. The sound is enhanced by the natural reverberations of the hall, just as your voice sounds better when you sing in the shower. Even in recording studios, almost every recording had artificial "echo" or reverberation added in the final mix, to simulate the live sound of a concert hall. So you can see that the "two-micro-

phone school" of thought has a lot going for it here—simple accurate reproduction unfettered by electronic interference.

There is a whole other school of thought that subscribes to a kind of modified studio approach. Although a large reverberant hall is still used as the recording location, a mixing console or remote truck will be brought along, and anywhere from eight to forty mikes will be in use. In smaller configurations, a stereo pair of mikes might be used for the overall pickup, with highlight, or spot mikes used on each section—first violins, seconds, violas, cellos, basses, woodwinds, brass, etc. More complicated setups will include a mike for every two wind players, and one each for percussion. In these situations, the stereo spread or panoramic perspective of the instruments is synthetically created by the use of the pan pots on the console, much as in pop recording. In essence, what's happening is that the production team uses studio recording techniques in a nonstudio situation and sacrifices the loss of control over leakage for the naturally good sound of the reverberant hall. This technique is very popular with Vanguard and Columbia records, among others, while the simpler two-mike technique can be heard to good advantage on Nonesuch, Gothic, Musical Heritage, Delos, Telarc, and a number of other small to medium-sized labels. Each technique has its own devotees, but a good engineer is aware of the respective advantages and disadvantages. As with any decision an engineer must make, it is important to choose the appropriate method keeping the final product, as well as the client's best interests in mind.

These two types of classical recording are most common and can be considered somewhat "purer" than the studio method. For recording large orchestral groups in the studio, an amazing amount of equipment is needed . . . headsets, microphones, inputs on the console. And the results can often sound a bit mechanical. Consequently, when orchestras are recorded in the studio, they are generally doing commercial jingles and movie soundtracks rather than artistic releases.

A large studio set up to record a vocal. Note the pads under mike stand to prevent vibration. (Courtesy Vanguard Studio—N.Y.C.

6 Rough Mixes

Back to the studio. "Rough" mixes, as opposed to final mixes, are done by an engineer or assistant engineer following a session or project, just to give a general idea of what's on the tape. Whereas a final mix would take hours to prepare, rough mixes take only a couple of minutes to make, and will probably be devoid of technical niceties. In general, then, when a client asks for a rough mix, he shouldn't expect to get fancy outboard effects such as digital delay or flanging, nor should he expect smooth fade-outs or noiseless tracks.

A word to assistant engineers: When you're given the opportunity to do rough mixes, you should consider them as important as finals. Here's your opportunity to see how good you can get it to sound in a hurry. Producers frequently call for rough mixes to be done between the time they finish playing and the time they're ready to leave the studio, which can be as little as twenty minutes. But it's not uncommon to expect—and get—rough mixes balanced, recorded on tape and cassette, leadered and boxed in that short a time. This is among the best training experience I know for assistants and junior engineers, and the single area where imperfection will be tolerated.

The rough mix will be used by the producer or artist for several purposes: to play the tracks for the record company to "hear how it's going in the studio," to hear at home in familiar surroundings how the studio is sounding, and to plan overdubs. On a rough mix, the producer will take note of all the subtleties the drummer might have played on the high hat, every lick the guitar player put in the fills, and every extension the pianist may have added to the basic lead-sheet chords. With this information, producer, artist, and arranger are better prepared to add horn, string, percussion, and vocal parts which will complement the existing rhythm tracks in the best way. Further down the line, a vocalist may want to hear "everything but the vocals" on a rough mix, so that he or she can play it at home and determine how the final vocal should be sung. Finally, a producer may want a rough mix of the finished multi-track master to plan for the final mix. This can save lots of expensive studio time, and is, in most cases, very worthwhile.

CASSETTES AND OPEN-REEL COPIES

Almost all studios are prepared to make ½-track or ¼-track open reel rough mixes for the client to take home. They can also put the mix simultaneously on a cassette, if necessary. Only the client knows which playback format he's most comfortable with out of the studio, and for what reasons. Some producers prefer cassettes so that they can listen in their cars. Some prefer open reel, so that they can sit at home and go over the tape, inch by inch, while planning the overdubs. Some people only *have* one or the other system, and are restricted by that limitation. In any event, multiple copies of a rough mix immediately after the session are usually very difficult to do. Because of the time crunch, the engineer wants to spend as much of the available time getting the mix to sound as right as possible, and as little time threading extra machines, patching them into the jack bay, and loading cassettes. If you can wait until the next day to get copies of your rough mix, you won't have any trouble . . . even if the studio manager has to stay up until dawn making them.

LISTENING AT HOME

Listening to rough mixes at home is a critically important step in the recording process. Most important, it lets you hear what you've done on a system with which you're familiar. Assuming you're happy with your system, it really doesn't matter if it's a terrific setup. As long as you're used to it and aware of any deficiencies it might have, you're in a position to make a decent judgment of sound quality. Don't make the mistake of complaining to the sound engineer that it doesn't sound as good at home as it did in the studio. It almost never will. That's why some very expensive mixes are done on some very cheap speakers. The theory here is that if it sounds good on cheap speakers it'll sound good on expensive ones. While this isn't always the case, there are a couple of cheap speakers that have become industry standards for the "cheap speaker sound." But at home you can compare the sound you're getting at the studio to some records you like and analyze some of the differences you might feel need correction. Is the bass muddy? Are the vocals too sibilant? Can you hear the strings as much as you'd like to? Does the snare drum have enough punch? These types of sound questions can be brought to the studio following the audition of a rough mix and dealt with by the engineer. Ultimately, if you're convinced that your listening situation is the ideal one, the studio may purchase speakers of the type you own so that you

Auratone
Sound Cubes

can best approximate your ideal when you mix. Or you can bring in your speakers from home.

ARRANGING AND PLANNING OVERDUBS

As mentioned before, rough mixes are ideal for planning overdubs. At this point the producer, artist, or arranger can write parts specifically tailored to the playing of the musicians on the rhythm track. A string line might be written to mirror a guitar fill; a horn rhythm might be written to balance a rigid drummer. A twelve-string guitar part might be added to fatten up the overall sound. Only now can you "see" what the finished product should sound like. The new ideas can be tried out at the piano while playing along with the rough mixes. Possible edits of the track may become apparent. In some cases the listener may realize that this track will never make it, no matter how many violins go on top of it, and decide to recut (re-record) the basic track. This is cheaper than having to hire a whole orchestra over again and is part of the reason why overdubbing became popular in the first place.

THE SOUND OF THE STUDIO

There is no ideal listening situation. Studios strive for two things. First, they want their control-room monitors to sound excellent. Second, they want that sound to "translate." The ultimate measure of a control-room environment is not how many gadgets it has in the rack, but how the sound translates to other systems. A tape from a good studio should be playable with all the values of the production intact on as many different systems as possible: in your home, in your car, in the record company's offices, or on your cassette machine. For this reason, many studios use identical speaker systems for control-room monitoring. The most common systems today include

Big Reds, Urei Time-Aligned, Altec 604's, JBL 4311, and the Auratone Sound Cubes.

But even considering the standardization among many studios, there remain some big sonic differences caused by the control rooms themselves. Every room will introduce a characteristic sound of its own. (Anechoic chambers are the only truly colorless rooms, and they are not found in recording studios. This is to say that if you mix on speaker "A" with preamp "B" and power amp "C" and then go home and play the mix over an identical system, it won't sound identical. This is because your living room is at least somewhat different from the control room at the studio. It's important to remember this when you listen to mixes, rough or final.

There are several ways to "standardize" a control room. These include the use of room equalization, reverberation, and the use of standard components, as mentioned above. Room equalization involves measuring the frequency response of the speakers at the "mixer position" and correcting any deficiencies with the use of a 1/3-octave graphic equalizer. This reshapes the sound contours to approach a standard "flat" frequency-response curve. (The common curve for home playback is not flat, and some speakers are adjusted to approximate home response rather than flat response.)

Reverberation analysis, a relatively new technique developed by Acoustilog, Inc., measures the time it takes for a sound to die away (also at the mixer position) in several different frequency bands. After interpreting the results of this analysis, the studio may need to change the acoustics of the control room. When they measure again, they hope that the reverberation response curve will indicate that the control room is now within "standard" parameters of response. Ideally, the room equalization takes place after the reverb analysis and correction has been done. These two techniques, combined with good-sounding, accurate reproducers, will yield the sound that translates best to other systems.

Monitors in a disc-cutting room.

There is another, cheaper technique in use, called "near-field monitoring." Near-field monitoring means simple placing the speakers very close to the mixing position to eliminate the influences of the acoustics of the direct sound from the speakers that there's no "room" left around for your ears for extraneous colorations. This technique is very popular in discos and in disco recording.

STANDARDIZING YOUR HOME

Forget it! Not only is it expensive, but you stand a good chance of alienating your mate, your neighbors, and yourself. The best compromise is to buy a pair of decent speakers (but not fabulous tri-amped electrostatic marvels) and put them in the living room. The room should not be very live, but not too dead either. Place the speakers six to ten feet apart and sit in the center so that you form an equilateral triangle with the two speakers. That's about as standard as you should need to get to hear tapes properly. As to the tape deck itself . . . read on.

HOME TAPE-DECKS

There are three formats to speak about here: open reel ½-track, open reel ¼-track, and cassette. You'll never get an 8-track cartridge from a studio, and rarely a full-track open-reel unless it's specifically requested. Your open-reel, home machine will have either a ½-track or ¼-track playback head and will probably run at 7½ i.p.s. The most common take-home rough mix is 7½ i.p.s. ¼-track. It will usually say what it is on the box. If the mix is recorded ½-track and you have a ¼-track playback system, there's no cause for alarm. The only practical difference in

your home playback will be in the relative levels of the two channels. This can be easily corrected by moving the balance control on your playback to the right, somewhere between 2:00 and 4:00, or until the sound is about equal from both speakers. On the other hand, if the tape is recorded ¼-track and your machine is ½-track, you're going to hear unwanted tape hiss and noise. So try to avoid ¼-track copies if you know you have a ½-track machine.

A studio will almost never record on both sides of a tape. They can't do it on ½-track anyway, and it's a pain to have to flip the tape over in a rushed rough mix. It also makes editing totally out of the question. If your machine can accommodate slightly better things, like ½-track playback, 15 i.p.s. speed, and Dolby A or dbx decoding, then request that your rough mix be made according to any of those. Except for the slightly less common dbx, they will present no problem at most studios.

If you require a cassette tape of your rough mixes, you need only specify that you want it with the built-in Dolby feature. The studio's cassettes are not likely to be the CRO2 type, so don't expect chrome unless you've asked for it specifically in advance of the session. Your tape copies may seem outrageously expensive, with cassettes running from $5 to $25 each and open-reel mixes going for the full studio rate plus the tape charge; but tape is a profit item for studios and is an integral part of their sales picture. Just as you'd pay more for a bottle of wine in a restaurant than in a liquor store, so it goes with tape in recording studios.

Now you've got a rough mix on tape to play at home: to listen to the sound of the studio, to arrange the overdubs, to edit from, to plan your moves for the final mix. Now let's go back into the studio and do it.

7 Overdubs

Since the invention of the SEL-SYNC (selective synchronization) process, overdubs have been an integral part of the recording business. In the days before sync, overdubs were done by recording the "instrumental" track on a ¼-inch mono tape and then playing that tape back to the singer to sing along with. The results were blended together onto a second tape recorder to achieve the final mix. In this way a number of vocal performances could be recorded over identical band "tracks." But since multi-track has become available, it's preferable to record one or more performances of the vocal on separate tracks of the same length of tape, and then pick and choose the best elements from all the performances to be mixed down to a two-track master tape.

Earlier on, we discussed overdubbing in disco recording, to achieve total isolation of tracks from one another. This is a long way from recording the whole band in mono and adding a vocal. Since overdubbing is an accepted part of studio procedure these days, it's a chapter (at least) all its own.

Assuming we have basic tracks recorded . . . bass, drums, keyboard, rhythm guitar . . . one might now consider overdubbing any of several things. A percussionist, a string or horn section, a group of vocalists for background, a solo lead vocal, or a solo/instrumental passage. Because there will be a small number of musicians present at most overdub sessions (with the exception of strings and horns) more time is usually spent in making these added tracks perfect. It's not uncommon to spend several hours getting a vocal right, or experimenting with a percussionist to achieve the ideal sound for the record. But since string and horn overdubs are the most "standardized" procedures, let's discuss them first.

String sections are often added to basic tracks and are called "sweetening" tracks. Strings are sometimes added not for their specific harmonic or melodic contribution, but for their softening effect on the overall texture of the sound. For this reason, string overdub is sometimes referred to as a "cushion." (As you can probably guess, this sort of playing isn't exactly a big thrill for the string players.)

String overdubs usually consist of a standard string section: violins, divided into two groups, violas, and cellos, with an occasional added harp. In the studio, each player is given a headset, preferably of the single-ear variety, so that the "open" ear can hear the rest of the group. The song to be "sweetened" is played back over the studio speakers while the conductor or concertmaster goes over the notes, form, and bowings with the section players. After the first playing, any questions about notes, phrasings, divisis, etc. are resolved and the section is ready to play the song down once with their headsets on and the speakers in the studio off. This "pass" at the song gives the engineer a very quick chance to get a balance on the string section, since the entire group will probably be locked into two channels of tape, no matter how many microphones are used. If all is going well, the engineer will be ready to record following this run-through. At this point, one or two tracks of the multi-track machine are placed into the record mode, and the string overdub is recorded.

After recording, the conductor and/or producer will ask for a playback. At the same time, the engineer will usually play back the track over the studio speakers for the players to hear. Between the producers and the musicians, you can be pretty sure that someone will dislike something. At this point, the producer will request another pass at the song so that the suggested refinements can be made. If everything goes well, that's the whole process. Union recording dates for string overdubs permit four songs to be sweetened in a three-hour period and there are several provisions regarding overtime. Ask your contractor.

Regarding the sound of a string overdub, a lush, sweet sound is achieved most easily by using a large number of players in a good, reverberant room. A typical string section for a record might consist of eight violins, four violas, and two cellos. In days gone by, when union scales were a lot lower, you might see forty string players on a date; but today's prices sometimes necessitate sections as small as six or eight players. The string parts should obviously be arranged before the session begins, and all parts copied out precisely and legibly. The actual recording techniques for strings vary somewhat, but strings are mostly recorded in large rooms with one mike for each pair of players, placed directly between them, and five or six feet high. Each cello or harp gets its own mike. Condenser mikes work very well with strings. Sometimes a stereo pair of mikes is used for an overall pickup, placed about ten feet high and six to ten feet in front of the ensemble. Gobos or baffles are rarely used, and, then only to isolate the harp from the rest of the section.

HORN OVERDUBS

Horn overdubs are similar to string overdubs, except that there's a bit more flexibility all around. One can have the horn charts arranged . . . and in that case the recording routine is the same as for the strings. The only differences are that the players may be more demanding about hearing themselves in the headsets, and they'll require a separate mike for each player. Horn sections can consist of a trumpet or two, a trombone or two, perhaps as many as four French horns, and a section of saxophones, ranging in size from soprano to baritone. A baritone sax part is sometimes written in place of the bass trombone, because its sound cuts through and lends more of a "punch" to the section's sound.

In a horn overdub, solos from within the group may or may not be played at the group session. Sometimes if a solo is difficult or improvised, it's better to have the soloist do a separate session or stay after the others have left. This minimizes the time in the studio for the group, saves money, and lets the horn players move up the street to the next job. In special cases, integrated horn sections like the Tower of Power or Brecker Brothers are asked to develop their own charts to go along with a song. The leader(s) of this kind of "horn machine" should be given cassettes of the rough mixes so that the section can develop its ideas prior to the overdub. Using integrated groups like this may cost more than hiring single players, but sometimes they yield a unique blend or a particular type of voicing or articulation that a "general" type of arranger might not conceive.

PERCUSSION OVERDUBS

Percussion overdubs are usually done with either one or two percussionists, and once again, the parts can be written out or left to the discretion of the percussionist. Most players who show up for an overdub session will come prepared with a "toy box" or trap case loaded with goodies . . . from tambourines to ratchets. It's best to let the musician know what type of sound you're looking for so he or she can bring the right instrument. Percussionists can be expected to play everything from congas to bongos, bells, chimes, cabasa, timpani, mallet instruments, bell tree, and sound effects. Percussion will be recorded on either one track or two, for a stereo spread. If several different instruments or patterns are involved, e.g., tambourine, congas, cuica, and timbales, a track or two will be needed for each sound.

BACKGROUND SINGERS

Background singers would be the next group to mention. In the ideal situation, background singers will blend perfectly, so that a single microphone can be used to pick them up and send them to one track on the tape. Happily, this is quite common. Only when it's impossible to get a blend does it become necessary to multi-mike and multi-track them for subsequent mixing and bouncing to a single track. But assuming they're blended well, background vocals are not hard to record. And I've always found background singers to be among the most accommodating of musicians.

In many cases, the singers will not know the parts when they arrive. A good approach then is to go over the written parts at the piano, demonstrating the individual lines; or let the singers hear the track several times to familiarize themselves with what and when they're supposed to sing. Again, a cassette before the session would not have hurt, but most studio singers can learn their parts pretty quickly.

Background vocals, like strings, are sometimes used as "cushions" rather than as distinctly heard accompaniments. For this reason, certain performance techniques become very important. The articulation of word beginnings is critical to a good ensemble attack, and sometimes it becomes necessary to leave off the end of a word so that the backgrounds blend back into the track when the lead vocal comes in. For example, if a group of singers is holding out the word "love" for two bars, it may be better if they leave off the ending "v" sound if it interferes with the lead. Excessive sibilance can also interfere with the track. Techniques for working with background vocals quickly become evident as a matter of necessity, and most background singers with any experience are well aware of what they have to do as long as you point out the problems.

Some engineers prefer to record background vocals (or any vocals for that matter) using the omnidirectional pickup rather than cardioid. This would tend to de-emphasize the bass boost introduced by the proximity effect, and help eliminate popped "p"s and "b"s somewhat. If however, the vocal is being sung in any kind of a live room, it may tend to lose "presence" (a word that makes engineers shudder). If there's a problem with presence, try putting the mike into cardioid pattern. If it's still a problem, follow the engineer's lead. Some re-equalizing, limiting, or repositioning of the vocalists might be in order.

INSTRUMENTAL SOLOS

Instrumental solos are technically simple to overdub. In most cases, one mike, one headset, and away you go. A trumpet or sax, flute or fiddle can be handled in this way. When it comes to electric guitar, several amplifiers may be tried in several positions in the room, depending on the type of music, but generally, instrumental overdubs don't present many technical problems. It may take hours to get the music to sound the way you want it, though. An instrumental solo is a sensitive thing. If the part is written, the difficulty is minimal; but for an improvised solo, the musician may want to make a few tries at each passage, without going on until he arrives at one he's happy with.

Making the producer, artists, and soloist all happy can be difficult. I've found two basic approaches that work for me. If you conceive of a certain instrument playing a certain line for a solo, write it out and hire a musician to play what's written. Then give him the opportunity to create a couple of solos. There's the chance that he may come up with something you like better than what you've written. The second approach is to hire a musician who has proven ability for the kind of music you're doing, and let him do his thing. Trying to "discuss" the improvisation with the musician in order to tailor it to your concept is usually a poor approach. A third approach is to let the musicians improvise several solos along the same melodic idea, record them all, and combine them to best musical advantage in the mix. This may not be the purest way to do it, since the solo concepts may be arbitrarily juxtaposed by you in ways that the musician might never have done it; but if it works for the end user, the producer, then it's good. It's nice to try and please everyone, but remember that the producer is responsible for the commercial success of the recording. If success is the goal of the recording, the producer is the vehicle.

VOCAL SOLOS

The lead vocal on a record is, with the exception of the song itself, by far the most important element in a recording session. It's got to be delivered in a way that's going to maximize the potential of the song. Sometimes lead vocals just pop out, like blossoms in the spring . . . and sometimes they have to be dragged out, like reluctant molars. In terms of studio time, lead vocals are the least consistent element in the recording process. A given song might take, literally, three minutes, or, more usually, a couple of hours. Sometimes a vocalist can keep trying for weeks to get it right. Along the way, there might be several performances that are very good, a couple that are excellent, and assorted pieces that can be patched together to make "the" vocal. Depending on your personality, your needs, and your budget, the final vocal that goes out over the air may be any of these things. Needless to say, it's best to work with a lead singer who has good technique, a reliable set of vocal cords, and a solid concept for the song.

THE PSYCHOLOGY OF OVERDUBBING

The idea in overdubbing is to get the best possible performance from the musician(s) involved. Depending on the situation, there may be a number of factors involved in getting that performance. If you have ever done an overdub yourself, you know what it feels like, but if not, try to imagine yourself in this situation.

You're all alone in a studio . . . just you and your in-strument. On the other side of the glass is an engineer, a producer and sometimes an assistant, an arranger, the artists, people from the record company, and heaven knows who else. You're expected to ignore all these people, except when one of them speaks to you over the talkback system and gives you instructions. You're likely to have a variety of feelings, ranging from hostility toward the people in the booth, to loneliness, to outright fright or frustration. Now you play your solo. The headphone balance isn't right, you can't hear yourself the way you thought you would, and the whole track sounds like hell. On top of all this, the guy inside wants you to play it like Charlie Parker or Duane Allman, or whoever. Although this picture seems bleak, it can very often be just this way.

It's the job of the producer and the engineer to try and eliminate some of the hazards presented to the musician in the overdub situation. Obviously, reducing the number of people around is a step in the right direction. It also seems to help to try and relax with the musician for a while before the playing starts. Play the song in the control room, discuss the desired effect of the overdub, have a cup of coffee, and, without being overly solicitous, try to communicate a relaxed, confident atmosphere. Even if the musician has never heard the song before, he or she is the "star" of the show for the moment, and should be made as comfortable as possible. Taking a moment to adjust the cue mix to the musician's taste, and adjusting the lights and the talkback volume to comfortable levels can go a long way toward getting an ideal performance. Once the atmosphere is established and everyone feels comfortable, the recording can begin in earnest.

There will be a need, in many instances, to "punch in" on a track. (Punch-in means re-recording a section of an overdub.) Let's say the first eight bars were sensational, but a wrong note was played in Bar 9. The engineer can play back the first eight bars and then put the tape deck in RECORD mode a fraction of a second before Bar 9 begins. (NOTE: this isn't always possible. Engineers like to have a beat of silence to punch in on, since punching on a sustained note hardly ever works.) Most tape decks have a locator function that enables the engineer to return to a programmed place on the tape any number of times until the "punch" is right. Naturally, if the wrong note occurs between two good sections of the solo, you'll have to "punch out" as you punched in. Again, it's good to have at least a beat's rest to do it in. Musicians are usually happy to punch in a phrase because it means they won't have to play the whole thing all over again. In an improvised solo, which is different every time, the original might have been lost if not for the ability to punch in.

There may come a time when you're about to run out of empty tracks. If you left four open tracks for a vocal, for example, and you have three good vocals, but not the "right one" yet, you'll be tempted to erase one of the good ones. The answer here seems to be what's called "bouncing tracks." In bouncing, two

Two vocalists on
one mike.

or more tracks of previously recorded material are combined onto one empty track. This means that the original tracks (which have been bounced) can be erased and used again for new material. You may choose to combine the best parts of those three "good" vocals onto one track, leaving you three more tracks to play with; or you may go another route and try to combine instruments that were previously on separate tracks. For example, you may have recorded the drums on six tracks. This might be the ideal time to bounce them down to three . . . or two or one, depending on your needs. You may have recorded several horn overdubs at different times and can now make a "section" out of them by combining them onto one track.

The actual technical process of bouncing is quite simple, but there are a couple of sacrifices. The first sacrifice is that the new balance between instruments on the bounce track will be "locked in." Once you decide on a balance, record it, and erase the old tracks, you're stuck with that balance. No more bringing up the second trombone or flute obligato. So be careful. The second sacrifice is that you are adding a generation of tape hiss to the bounce track, since it consists of other played-back tracks. In most modern studios, this additional noise will not be noticeable, but it is worth bearing in mind. Bouncing tracks is another reason to be thankful for studios' noise reduction systems such as Dolby or dbx. They help to minimize the noise inherent in the transfer process.

OVERDUBS: WHY AND HOW MANY

This is basically a producing discussion, and there is no one answer. If you've got a cooking rock band that sounds great on stage, you may not need to overdub at all. If it's a jazz band or a classical string quartet, you'll almost certainly not need to overdub. But in a more common popular music setting, some overdubbing is almost always called for. The reasons, as mentioned before, include isolation, artistic control, creation of a mood, and availability of the musicians you need to overdub. That takes care of the why. As to the "how many," the only answer can be: "Just enough to make the record sound right." As many records have sounded bad because of too many overdubs as too few. Perhaps more. The term "overproduced" sometimes refers to an elaborate use of musicians on a record beyond what's actually necessary for the song. Though it might be tempting to have a percussionist lay down separate tracks for congas, bongos, shaker, berimbau, cuica, maracas and vibraslap, you may find your playbacks beginning to sound like a street band. Of course, if you've got unlimited money for musicians and studio time, you can always remove the superfluous overdubs before you mix. And it's tempting, as long as they're there, to double and triple the strings, to have the vocalists do just one more set of "shoo-wops," or to let the percussionist go wild; but more often than not, recording

time spent on impulse winds up being left out of the mix. This is not meant to stifle anyone's creativity but rather to put in a good word for planning ahead.

WHEN TO OVERDUB WHOM

This is pretty simple. The most common situations should have the rhythm section recorded first with a scratch vocal. At this point, any "fixing up" might be done to the rhythm parts: correct a wrong note in the bass, add a rhythm part on the 12-string guitar, and so on. At the subsequent session, either directly after the rhythm or, most likely, at a later date, the strings, then the horns, the background vocals, the percussion, and finally the solos and lead vocals can be recorded. Any of these groups can be overdubbed at any time, but this represents an ideal not often possible. In commercial jingles, for instance, the strings and horns may be recorded at the same time. The philosophy is that you want to have as much of the orchestration available to the overdubbing musicians as is needed. String players will be happy with just rhythms and vocal, for example; whereas a guitar soloist might want to have rhythm, vocal, strings, horn and backgrounds to fit his solo in best. For the final vocal, even if the artist wants to hear just the original rhythm section in the cue, it's best to have everything else on tape.

CLEANING UP THE TRACKS

This is a housekeeping type of chore done with the engineer. Cleaning up tracks can include doing bounces after all the musicians have gone home. It can also include spot erasing . . . where the trumpet player sneezed during a four-bar rest, where the vocalist coughed while waiting to come in, etc. If the tracks are clean, i.e. nothing's there but the right music at the right time, it's possible to leave faders open during a mix. If they're not cleaned, you'll be doing a lot of muting, or shutting off tracks, when the coughs or false entrances come up during the mix. It may seem a "waste" of good studio time for something that doesn't involve actually recording or mixing music, but cleaning up the tracks will save you lots of headaches when it comes time to mix the record.

THE NEXT ROUGH MIX

After the overdubs are done, the artist has laid down the perfect lead vocal, and the last cough has been erased during the cleanup, it's time to take home the last rough mix. At this point, everything is on the tape that's going to be on the record except for special effects which will be added during mixing. It's at this point that the producer and artist can reflect on what they've got. Does it work? Did it go as planned? Is it a hit? Shall we add another solo line? Should we drop the background vocals on the second chorus? All these and a million more questions have to be dealt with at this time, prior to the mixing sessions. Sure, you can always remix, but the idea is to get it as right as possible the first time. The rough mix you take home at this point should be well balanced and should approximate, if only somewhat, the sound of the final recording. Here it's appropriate to consider the possibilities of all the outboard signal processing equipment at your disposal in the studio. Your record may sound just great the way it is, and there will be no need for outboards, but if you want

them, you can choose from a virtual sea of toys. Outboard equipment commonly found in big studios and often in small ones includes digital delay lines, echo chambers, flangers, phasers, noise gates, limiters, compressors and a variety of equalizers and filters. There's a whole list of less frequently used equipment, too! Echoplexes, ring modulators, bandpass filters, notch filters, parametric equalizers, stereo synthesizers . . . the list goes on. While you're listening to this last rough mix, you'll be thinking about some of these devices and making decisions, if only temporarily, about their use during the mix.

8 Mixing

Trying to understand the nature of mixing music is about as difficult a subject as life itself. (Well, perhaps a bit easier!) The blending of various sounds into a cohesive combination that satisfies commercial, musical, artistic, sonic, technical, and personal criteria is without question an art unto itself. It's widely known in the recording business that it takes at least five years to become a mixer, and even then, some people will never make it. The final mix, the purvue of the producer and the engineer, can be very ordinary, or it can raise the original musical material to heights never imagined by the artist. For these reasons, mixing can be at once the most flexible and difficult act in the creation of a recording.

THE TRANSPARENT ENGINEER

The goal of most classical music, jazz, authentic folk, and some rock recording is to present an image of the music free of influence of the medium of recording itself. That is to say, the engineering, the microphones, the tape recorders, the console, and the disc-mastering process should not be apparent to the listener. The idea is to place the listener as intimately as possible in relation to the performance. Recording engineers go to painstaking lengths toward this end. The use of transformerless preamps, noise reduction systems, high-speed transports, digital recording techniques, and single-vantage mike placement all contribute to a "transparent" recording. The reward is then to be recognized for not being transparent. If the kind of music you're recording requires this type of transparency, you'll need a minimum of equipment to do the job, but it should be of exceedingly high quality. There are specialty engineers around the country and around the world who do this type of recording extremely well, as evidenced by the hgh quality of classical recordings heard today. As I noted in an earlier chapter, there are several techniques for recording a "true" representation of a performance; but given a good hall and a well-balanced group of musicians, two mikes and a good tape deck with professional noise reduction will yield an excellent sound in almost every case.

THE CREATIVE MIX

Anything other than this kind of "representational" recording employs and demands a certain degree of creativity on the part of the engineer and producer.

Even if they're only concerned with stereo placement (panning) and adding artificial reverberation, decisions must be made regarding these factors. Going back to our "standard" pop recording, the mix will require, even in its most elementary form, the balancing of instruments and voices with respect to loudness, stereo placement, and adding reverberation to create an acoustic perspective. The basic ideas for these elements will come from the producer in most cases, with some suggestions made by the engineer. A number of producers like to have the engineers "set up the mix." Then the producers make suggestions to refine the sound to their liking. This is almost always a good way to start. Assuming the engineer has recorded the music, or has at least familiarized himself with the contents of the tape, his experience will generally speed up the process. The producer is then freed to concentrate on more subtle refinements of the mix. At any given time, the engineer might suggest using one or more outboard devices to enhance the sound. Most producers will at least listen to the altered sound and then decided whether or not to use it. Since producers are not primarily concerned with the technical end of a recording, they can't be expected to know the capabilities of every piece of outboard equipment and mixing techniques. Thus, the engineer tends to participate extensively in the mixing process.

Creative mixing can be a simple process in a multitrack situation, resulting in three or four jingles an hour. Or it can be as complex as brain surgery, involving computer storage of information, updating previous mixes to accommodate new ideas, scrapping whole sound-concepts for new ones, and creating a mood for a piece of music. Whatever the steps that the producer and engineer go through, their aim is to make the multi-track master into a two-track tape representing the best possible combination of sounds.

BABES IN TOYLAND

The recording studio's control room can be viewed as a sort of audio toy chest. Many producers, artists, arrangers, and engineers in early stages of their careers want to try everything in the room on their mixes. Frequently, they'll bring in things that the control room doesn't already have, or request that they be rented for the mixing sessions. There's nothing inherently wrong with this. Sometimes a special effect or two is needed; but the vast majority of first timers I've worked with tend to go way overboard in their explorations and use of outboard gear. I mention this only as a sort of warning to be aware of the situation. It's almost axiomatic that first-time producers and artists ask for too much echo. Confronted with a $6000 echo-plate or digital reverb, they get carried away with the sound they may want more than is actually appropriate for the music. I've heard new recording artists asking for everything from flanging on all the tracks to enough echo to make the tape sound like it was recorded in the men's room at Grand Central Station. Suffice to say that if you're new to studio experience, the best thing to do is to listen to the advice of the engineer and try to keep a realistic perspective on your desires, because certain elements and parameters of record-making have to be adhered to for any success at all.

SOME ELEMENTS OF MIXING

Mixing means blending all the sounds you've got on your multi-track master into a two-channel stereo quarter-inch tape. The two-channel tape is later played back for transfer to lacquer disc, which is then used in the creation of metal parts resulting in finished records. We'll discuss the mastering process later on in the book, but for now, the goal is the two-track tape. Once the multi-track tape has been brought up on faders with the console in a mixing configuration, you can begin to evaluate what you've got.

You'll probably listen to each instrument individually, and in the case of one instrument on several tracks (drums, for instance) listen to each track individually. At this stage, you can attempt to get a balance on the rhythm section and make corrections with the console's equalizers with reference to each channel on the tape. It may be that the high hat needs to be brought out more, so some high frequency equalization may be added. Perhaps the maracas sound too jangly, and some midrange (around 4 kHz) may be lessened (rolled-off) to achieve a smoother, more integrable sound. If the bass guitar isn't clear, it may require somewhat less in the bottom end, or more in the lower midrange for clarity of articulation. It may need limiting or compression (restriction of dynamic range) so that it feels like it's a constant presence under the band. There are hundreds of considerations in equalizing a program for mixing. If the tape was recorded with extensive equalization, you may find that very little is necessary during the mixing stage. Some engineers and producers prefer to equalize during the recording process. The philosophy is, "If it sounds right going in, it'll sound right coming out." This technique has the advantage of making mixing a little simpler, and saving additional noise from signal processing during the mix. The disadvantages are there as well. Once you've "dumped" the bottom from an electric bass, for example, you can't really put it back in the mix. In

Outboard equipment in low rack.

other cases, producers and engineers prefer to use "survival" equalization in recording, and save the refinements for mixing. With survival eq, obvious equalization problems will be eiminated in the recording sessions, such as an boomy bass, dull-sounding snare drum, or sibilant vocal; but the subtler points are left for later.

Once you've come to terms with equalization of the music, at least in a fairly specific sense, you'll continue to try different balances of the instruments with each other . . . more drums, less horns, more background vocals, less rhythm guitar . . . and so on. You have by now listened to your rough mixes, have a fairly good idea of the balances you want to hear, and can, as the tape is played back over and over again, begin to add echo (reverberation) and create new spatial relationships from front to back using different echo chambers. After several passes at the tape, getting the balances, eq, echo, and panning the way you want them, you'll begin to hear that the mix is going to sound exactly the way you wanted it to . . . or it's not. Usually, if it's not, you begin to experiment with outboard equipment. (I'm assuming that the performance you're after is there, and only sonic considerations are lacking.) You may find that phased cymbals, digital delay on the strings, or doubling a vocal electronically will produce what you want.

OUTBOARDS

In order to achieve some of these magical effects, audio technology has developed a vast number of signal processing devices, commonly referred to as outboard equipment, or simply, outboards. They're outboards because they're not in the board (console)

itself. Common outboard signal-processing devices include filters, equalizers, noise gates, limiters, expanders, phasers and flangers, digital and analog delay lines, reverberation chambers, pitch-change and noise reduction devices. Some highly specialized studios will include other outboards which may be either the musical-instrument-type accessory, such as an Echoplex, band pass filter (wah-wah), fuzz box, or synthesizers-type components such as ring modulators, sequencers, function generators, or vocorders.

Clearly, the options for signal processing are many. There are recordings made with little or no signal processing, but in some cases the producer will want to use many of the "black boxes" in the control room. Here's how some of those devices are used:

Filters can be used to remove whole sections of fundamentals or overtones from a given audio signal. *High-pass filters* (also known as *low-cut filters*) are most commonly used. As the name suggests, they let all the highs above a selected frequency "pass." The reciprocal variety of filter would be a *low-pass* (or *high-cut*) *filter*. High-pass filters are used to remove excessive low end such as might result from turntable rumble. Low-pass filters might be used where there is excessive hiss. The *notch filter* is used to remove a bandwidth of audio signal from other than the extreme ends of the audio spectrum. For example, you might need to "notch out" a problem sound at around 2kHz but leave the surrounding frequencies intact. Notch filters, with variable Q (bandwidth around the selected frequency) facilitate this technique. Commonly used filters are made by Pultec and UREI.

Equalizers are tone controls used to shape the frequency-response curve of a given signal, or in musical terms, to change its timbre. Although there are equalizers in each module of the console, outboard equalizers are sometimes used because they offer an additional selection of frequencies or a particular sound quality. Commonly used outboard equalizers are made by Neve, Pultec, and Auditronics.

Noise Gates cause any signal below a preset threshold of amplitude to be removed entirely. The use of a noise gate, referred to as "gating," can be pragmatical when you need to quiet down a noisy track below the level of the music; or creative—when you need to create a "punch" on a bass drum. The combined use of a compressor with a noise gate can yield a bass-drum sound with maximum impact and no decay.

Limiters and compressors are used to restrict dynamic range of a signal. They are needed when the natural dynamic range of an instrument or voice exceeds the capabilities of the tape, and the engineer is not able to "ride gain" incessantly. They are desirable, although not essential, in cases where a signal level should remain fairly constant irrespective of fluctuations in the actual dynamics of the performance. For example, a lead vocal may have a wide range and need to retain presence throughout the song so that the words don't get buried by the horn section. A compressor or limiter/compressor will help

achieve this. Commonly used limiters and compressors are made by UREI, Teletronix, Neve, and Allison Research.

Expanders work to restore dynamic range to a signal presenting insufficient range. Expanders can be used for special effects or for trying to stretch the dynamic range of a previously compressed signal.

Phasers and Flangers are special effects devices which cause a signal to exhibit a characteristic sound. The sound has been described as being like a jet plane passing overhead. If you can imagine that sound applied to a musical line, you can imagine the effect. Phasers and flangers can be adjusted for "depth" and "speed" of the effect. Commonly used phasers and flangers are made by MXR and Eventide.

Digital and Analog delay lines are used to create repetitions of the original signal. A repetition which occurs very shortly after the original (under 30 milliseconds) "thickens" the sound without the ear perceiving a distinct repetition. Longer delays are used for "doubling" (also known as ADT or automatic double tracking) where you might want to make a voice sound like two voices, or for making eight voices sound like sixteen. Digital or analog delays can also be used to delay the onset of reverberation, replacing the "tape slap" technique. Digital delay lines are preferred for studio use over analog because they have better noise specifications and better frequency response in the longer delays. Some delay lines have a "spin" or "regenerate" control which feeds the output signal back to the input, creating a long decay (reverberation) or a series of distinct repetitions, depending on the other settings on the DDL. Made by Eventide and MXR.

Reverberation chambers come in several types: live, plate, spring, and electronic (digital). A live chamber is a reverberant room with a speaker at one end and a microphone at the other. The "send" signal is played through the speaker, bounces around the reverberant room, and is picked up by the mike at the other end. The reverberant sound is then fed back to the console's "echo return" buss. Plate echo creates its reverberation using a large (4'x8') metal plate, which vibrates according to the signal fed into it. Spring reverb sends the signal along a coiled spring which is suspended between two posts. Digital reverb, which is relatively new, completely synthesizes reverberation using a microprocessor, and uses neither mechanical nor acoustical means whatsoever. Reverberation is used to enhance the sound of music in general, or to simulate the natural ambiance of a concert hall or auditorium. The most popular reverberation device is the EMT plate. Another plate-type device is manufactured by ECOPLATE. Spring reverb devices vary in quality and price, and are manufactured by AKG, Quad Eight, Orban, Fairchild, MXR, and others. Digital reverb is currently made by EMT and Lexicon. Live chambers you make yourself.

Pitch change devices are used to create harmony for an existing musical line, to change the overall

Clockwise from top left:
Eventide's Omni-pressor: Multi-faceted outboard.

Eventide's Flanger.

24 tracks of Dolby noise-reduction.

A very popular pitch change device: Model H 949 Harmo-nizer.

Eventide Digital Delay Line 1745 M.

Noise Gates by Allison Research (Valley People) and Roger Mayer.

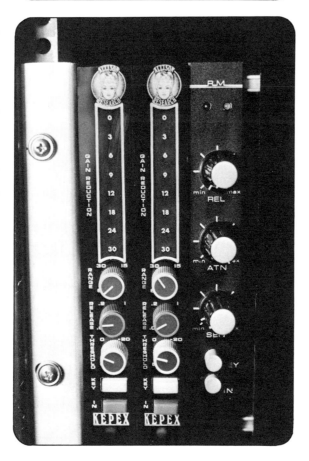

pitch and quality of a signal, or for correcting out of tune playing. The first two are easy and fun to experiment with. The last is hard to do and no fun at all. By far the most common and popular pitch change device is the Eventide Harmonizer.

Noise reduction devices are used to prevent tape hiss from ever reaching your ears. By compressing and expanding certain frequencies during recording and playback, these devices "push" the tape hiss below the level of audibility. The Dolby "A" system is almost universally used in recording studios, and the dbx system has some popularity. Engineers have mixed opinions about both systems. Some people feel that they add color to the sound which is processed through them. My feeling is that they are, when properly calibrated, a gift from heaven.

COMMON MISTAKES

We've already dealt with the "Babes in Toyland" syndrome, so you know to be aware of that. Another very common mistake in mixing is to want each instrument to be louder. Obviously, if you make each track louder, the overall level of the mix will be raised. Assuming the original mix was set to be within certain limits of loudness, you're probably pushing the needles on the VU meters farther than they want to go. A little technical info here: no matter how loud you may play the mix in the control room, the meters on the output of the console and the meters on the 2-track tape deck reflect the amount of signal being fed from console to recorder. In most cases, the machinery and the engineer would like to see the needles averaging around the "zero" point on the meter, where the line turns red. VU meters are averaging meters, which means they don't respond to peaks in the loudness of the signal. The zero point refers to maximum average modulation of the signal within the specified limits of the equipment being used. If your meters are constantly "in the red," it probably means that you are overmodulating or printing too hot. Although most consoles have enough "headroom" and tape and tape recorders can accommodate excessive levels for short periods, it's usually best to keep out of the red for more than brief periods of dynamic excitement. Going too far in the other direction, or recording at a low level, is going to result in the mix's not being hot enough, and will add some noise from the tape itself, which wouldn't have been apparent if the mix had been done at a higher level. Some engineers love to "print hot" and hardly pay attention to the meters. This often results in distortion of the signal. It may not be immediately apparent that this distortion is occuring, but the laws of physics assure us that it's there. The idea is that a hotter tape will result in a hotter recording, which will reduce tape noise, sound louder on the radio, and get more attention from the listener. In practical reality, however, you should know that radio stations employ compressors in their broadcast equipment which ensure that almost everything they play will be as hot as possible, and at the same time not permit any one record to be any louder than another. So unless the engineer presents a convincing argument to the effect that the meters don't mean anything to your mix, or you are, in fact, after a somewhat distorted sound, it pays to keep an eye on the meters. Just as a sideline, it's been said that digital recording is "too clean" for some artists. They may have become used to the inherent distortion present in analog tape-recording and it's sort of "grown" on them. The kind of distortion I'm speaking of is fairly subtle. The more obvious type, which is clearly audible as "breaking up" or a sort of "smashed" abrasive sound, is due to overloading of a preamp somewhere down the line (frequently at the microphone preamp or the preamp of a guitar or bass amplifier) or to the serious misalignment of a tape recorder. Under no circumstances should you accept this sound on your tape. Even if the people on the studio staff are hard pressed to explain its presence, you shouldn't continue until the situation has been corrected. One nasty thing about distortion is that once it's on the tape, you'll never be able to get rid of it. Forget about fixing it in the mix.

In most cases, engineers are aware of the tendency to push levels up and will warn you that you're getting too hot for the tape. At this point, you can back down all your channels somewhat and turn up the monitor level, if you like. If there's a "perfect" balance between the input faders that you absolutely can't disturb, it's sometimes permissible to bring down the overall level of the mix with the master fader. This is the two- or four-gang fader, which is the last stage before the signal leaves the board and goes to the two-track recorder. If you find yourself constantly pushing up the input faders and then constantly lowering the master fader, though, you'll be interfering with the ideal gain structure of the console and detracting from an optimum sound.

If you feel this happening, you're probably not monitoring properly. This may be the fault of the room or your mixing technique. Try taking a rest and asking the engineer for his ideas on the situation. He may suggest monitoring on a set of small, radio-like speakers and listening at a "normal" level, rather than as loud as it's been. Remember that it's very tempting to hear your tape played loud, but it's not ideal for actually mixing. When a tape is played extremely loud, the frequency response of the music will appear to change, due to the Fletcher-Munson effect. This means that the ear's sensitivity to frequency response differs at different amplitude levels; or to put it very simply, highs and lows are exaggerated at loud levels. Also, your ears actually begin to act as "limiters." This is your body's way of protecting itself from physical injury.

If the reason you've been pushing faders so much is that you just can't seem to hear it right, perhaps the acoustics of the control room are not suitable for mixing your music. There are two choices here. Either move to another studio, or listen on small speakers at fairly close range. Near-field monitoring at a decent level helps to eliminate control-room acoustics and lets you hear the "direct" sound from the speakers. This will frequently eliminate the problem. Many producers have favorite rooms for mixing. Some of the best studios around are simply unlucky in that they can't present an ideal mixing environment, although they may be fabulous for recording. This is sometimes why you'll see separate credits on an album for recording and mixing. (Although this is just as often a matter of politics and personal interests.)

Another common mistake occurs in fading out a mix. You may be tempted to let a song fade over many seconds, until it disappears at the last possible moment. Muscially, this may be terrific, and the slow fade has been used to excellent advantage at times. Practically, though, remember that a radio station will jump in with a commercial or throw a program back to the announcer long before your fade has ended. The best fades get in as much of the "meat" as possible in a relatively short period. This is not to say that the song should sound like it fell off a cliff, but a brief, tasteful fade is important for successful segues on the radio. If your song ends with a "vamp" or repetition of a musical subject, no one wants to hear it repeated ten times because the guitar finally got hot on the last repeat. Better to edit the tape so that the "hot" lick occurs earlier in the fade.

Mixing for too long a period of time can be another minus factor. Whether it's working on one song or several, the ear and your concentration will begin to flag after several hours. Just as you were fresh for the recording, you want to be fresh for the mixing. Since mixing usually requires very intense concentration, it's best done in reasonably short periods. On every pass of the tape, you're concentrating on one or another instrument for level, color, echo, eq, and to determine that it's fitting into the overall mix. You may suddenly find that you've gone through a whole pass concentrating on the drums and have not even noticed the other instruments. It's amazing, but it happens. It's most important to be able to maintain a degree of objectivity in mixing. In ten years of mixing records, I have found that when I have worked too long, I become bored with the music; I want to go home, and I get "expedient," I'll begin to be short with people I'm working with and tend to compromise what I think might be best for the project. Obviously, this isn't going to get me a lot of work with people who like to work all through the night; but it's fact. There are some engineers who can comfortably spend ten or twelve hours mixing. But you should consider the engineer's needs and patterns when you're mixing. Although you may be excited about the project and running on adrenalin and able to mix for 44 hours in a row, consider that the engineer has been here before and will return to work here after your project is done. Recording and mixing engineers are unusually good about sharing your spirit and enthusiasm, but bear in mind that they're

human and need food, rest, and regularity in their lives. They'll appreciate your consideration and your tape will undoubtedly sound better.

MONITORING YOUR MIX

It's usually delightful to listen to your music played loud over the studio monitors. During recording, overdub sessions, or just simple playbacks in the studio for musicians, friends or interested record company executives, this is obviously the way to go. Nice big speakers with a powerful amplifier will show the tape to good advantage and make the whole crowd feel good. But mixing isn't supposed to make you feel good; it's a time to get the music right. Since you must assume that your listeners at home and in the car aren't going to hear the music over such an impressive system, you must deal with the realities of the common listening situation. With respect to volume, you've got to assume that most people will be hearing the music in the car or in a situation at home where the equipment is "average" and the listener's concentration is minimal.

With these factors in mind, you can assume that the average listening level will be low to moderate. Even with music that is designed to be heard loud. such as disco or rock, the general population is not willing to risk an apartment lease or a pair of eardrums for the sake of the music. Remembering the Fletcher-Munson effect and the average listening situation, you'll see some wisdom in preparing a mix under somewhat more standard conditions.

SPEAKERS AND AMPLIFIERS

Once again, a $2000 pair of speakers powered by 600 watts of clean amplification is going to sound pretty spectacular compared to a home or car setup. For this reason, most studios offer at least one set of alternative speakers for mixing. Most often, a pair of moderate-sized bookshelf-type speakers will be available, and probably a small pair of Auratone Sound Cubes or a similar type will be there as well. Think of the bookshelf speakers as being the "home," and the Auratones as the "car." Ideally, the studio monitors should translate well to the bookshelf speakers and the Auratones. Although the big speakers will probably have been equalized and the control room analyzed for acoustic response, and although the two smaller sets of speakers will not have the benefit of these technologies, most studios try to make the sound very close so that there are no surprises when you change speakers, other than the obvious color and level shifts inherent in smaller speakers.

If you're mixing mono, one speaker is all you need, and usually the small one is best. Mono is used for commercial jingles, film tracks, and some (rare) single records. Bear in mind that AM radio has only recently been licensed to broadcast in stereo and is often still set up only for mono. Most large FM stations broadcast in stereo, however. In most cases, though, you'll be mixing in stereo.

The ideal placement for the listener in stereo mixing is at the apex of an equilateral triangle with the speakers. If you're too far to the left or right, the mix will sound unbalanced, and you'll be tempted to restructure the mix to suit your position. The best position for the speakers is one that allows both the producer and the engineer to be fairly close to the middle of that equilateral triangle. Occasionally, you may find it useful to sit or stand directly behind the engineer, who has located himself in the best position for working.

As to the actual speakers, several brand names are popular in studios. For the main monitors, look for UREI, Altec, Big Reds, and JBL's, in the United States. For the bookshelf type, you can expect to see JBL's again (models 4311 and 4313 are common), KLH, AR's, and Little Reds. For the mini-speakers, Auratones are almost universally used, followed by Secret Sound Cubes, and others by ADS, Braun, Colbert, and Technics. In some cases, studios even rig the console output up to an actual portable radio speaker that sits on the producer's desk. In terms of amplification in the control room, rest assured that a studio that has spent at least $100,000 and possibly $500,000 getting itself together will have a few good amps around. Common brands include Crown, Mac-Intosh, Dyna, BGW, and Phase Linear, and they'll all be matched to the efficiency of the speakers they drive.

9 Editing

When it comes to editing, I can be fairly clear about techniques, because there are only a couple. Editing is the physical rearrangement of sections of tape, and is basically done in two ways . . . electronically and mechanically. Electronic editing is the accepted method in videotape, since cutting videotape with a razor blade yields unsuccessful edits. Electronic editing in audio is rare, unless one considers punching-in to be editing. Mainly, what we're discussing is using a razor blade to cut out an unnecessary piece of tape. Editing is done on all forms of audio tape, from the 2" multitrack master down to the ¼" mix tape. To understand the process, a bit of background is necessary.

Sound is represented on a piece of tape as electromagnetic signals recorded in a real time sequence. As the tape is played back, it's passed across the REPRODUCE head (playback head) on the tape deck. This head begins the translation of the magnetic signals into audible music or speech, called audio. In order to determine where an edit is to begin, the engineer locates the specific point on the tape by moving it slowly across the playback head. He then marks the spot on the outside of the tape with a grease pencil in most cases, and proceeds to find and mark the point at which you want to rejoin the original tape program. With both points marked, he then physically cuts out the undesired length of tape with a razor blade and rejoins the two loose ends with a piece of special adhesive tape called *splicing* tape. The rejoined ends of the tape are called a *splice*.

A typical music editing situation might be as follows: You've recorded a rhythm track, and upon playing it back a number of times, have determined that it's just too long for the song or its potential radio play. You may decide that you don't need the entire third chorus of the song . . . or the bridge . . . or the introduction. If an edit is technically feasible, the engineer can simply cut the unwanted part, splice the loose ends, and wind up with a shorter version of the song that fits your needs.

Another example: In speech editing, a mainstay of commercially oriented studios doing industrial , radio, TV, and filmstrip work, it's almost always necessary to edit an announcer's performance. He may have had a slip of the tongue, coughed, asked a question, or mispronounced a word. By editing the tape to match exactly what's on the script, the end result is what sounds like a perfect rendition of the copy (script). Frequently, a tape editor is called upon to "pace" an announcer or interview tape. In this type of editing, the editor takes out and adds blank space where needed to create a smooth, flowing narration or dialog. In these cases, blank tape is not used to add time, but rather tape which has recorded "room tone" on it. Room tone is the sound of the studio with the microphone on and no one in the room. In other words, it's how the room would sound during a natural silence. There's an audible difference between room tone and blank tape. Some room tone is used in classical music records instead of leader tape between

Two-inch editing block with leader tape.

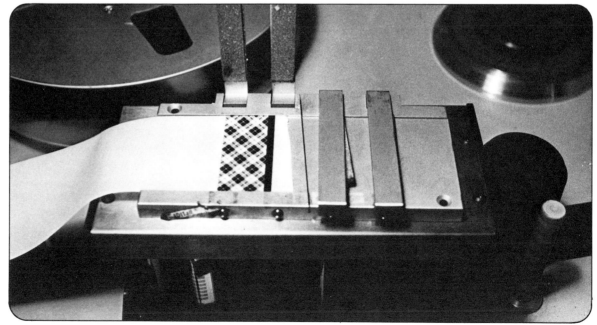

selections, to give the aural impression of a continuous live performance.

Getting back to music, here's another example of an edit: the introduction and first chorus of a song are excellent from Take 1, and the second chorus and ending are better from Take 4. It may be possible to splice these together to make a perfect whole take on two conditions: First, the tempos on both sides of the potential splice must be exactly the same. It's no good to have two great performances to splice together if one is noticeably faster than the other. Second, it's essential that the pitch is correct. Some instruments go either flat or sharp after a while, and it's possible that a band's intonation will change from Take 1 to Take 4. It's occasionally possible to correct pitch, but only on one or two tracks at a time, using a pitch-change device such as the Eventide Harmonizer. But this is a remedial approach which is often difficult and unsatisfactory. If you find yourself anticipating some multi-track editing, two devices can be of some help: the click track and the strobe tuner. A click track (digital metronome) can be used, either throughout the recording or as a count-off, to ensure uniform tempo from take to take. For pitch, the musicians can tune up to the piano or to a strobe tuner before each take. Uniformity of tempo and pitch will make edits a lot easier.

There are other criteria to meet though. In order for an edit to work, that is to be imperceptible, there should be no long decays across the splice. The dying away of a cymbal crash is the worst offender. Similarly, if the bass player plays a descending run in Take 1, but with a different rhythmic figure in Take 4, the splice may be musically awkward. All these factors must be considered when evaluating a splice. Some engineers don't like to splice over sustained notes in strings, horns or vocals, because the actual level and intensity of the held note on each side of the splice is rarely exactly the same, and minor differences are exaggerated by a splice of this type. If you've tried a splice and it doesn't work, you can always put back the missing piece (save those pieces!) and try to splice at another point. If the downbeat of a chorus is not good for editing purposes, it's possible that the beat before or the beat after will work better. It would be ideal if all your edits worked, but some never will. In planning an edit, try to make sure that you're prepared for the possibilities mentioned. In recording, if you're going to make a new ending without playing the whole song over again, it's a good idea to play the chosen take back to the musicians for a little while so that they can get the tempo and feel right. And remember about those decays!

In some cases, when you're sure about the basic factors, you might wait until after the mix to do your editing for several reasons. First, it's physically easier to edit ¼" tape than it is to edit 2", and it takes much less time per edit. Second, for the budget-minded, 2" tape (or any tape for that matter) can be erased and used again at a later date if it's free of splices. Some people prefer to go this route and re-

use their multi-track tape for different projects. The theory here is that once the mix is completed and the record's been made, the two-track master is all that will be necessary for the future, so why not erase the multi-track and use it again? Since 2" tape costs between $100 and $150 per reel in the studio, this method is worth some consideration if you're paying the bills. But several words of warning: Once it's gone, it's gone. You can never remix that multi-track, so be sure you love your mix. For a "hit" type of artist, the multi-track tape may be needed at some future time for remixing a mono version, for transfer to film, to make "TV tracks" (all the instruments, but no lead vocal, so the singer can appear singing "live" on a TV show with the tape played behind him), or for remixing for an anthology type of record . . . "The Best of Joe Hit." In an anthology, the record company might want to remix all the tunes, recorded at different times in different studios, for a more uniform sound than could be had by just splicing together copies of the various two-track masters. So try to look toward the future if you plan to re-use tape.

Some studios will permit bulk-erased tape to be used for an original recording session, provided it's of the type for which their machines are aligned. But most studios discourage the use of used tape, especially if it has splices in it, because it's very chancy to record over a splice and expect uniform results. Some studios don't permit you to bring your own tape, used or new, because the sale of tape is part of their profit picture.

WHAT EDITING CAN'T DO

Editing is an essentially simple process which can be used to correct some errors in performance or recording. Editing can not work laterally. That is, you can't take the guitar solo off Take 1 and put it over the rhythm section in Take 4. When you edit, you move everything that's happening on the tape at that instant in time. In order to make a lateral edit, you'd require two multi-track machines, sync information printed on both tapes, a Harmonizer, and a lot of patience. An edit of this type is really an overdub by a machine. For that to work, both machines must run at exactly the same speed. The only way to achieve this is to link the movement of their transports together, which requires extra equipment, time, and money. With the right tools, a lateral edit can occasionally be done by an excellent engineer who happens to be very lucky that day; but it's not something you want to count on.

There are edits which just won't work. In those cases, you can experiment till the cows come home, but to no avail. Remember to plan the edits. Always record a few extra measures in front of and after the edit points you plan to take, use the click track and strobe tuner, and play back the good take when recording an insert so the musicians can get the feel again.

10 Mastering

The master lacquer is the first "record" that's cut using your two-track master tape. If you're recording a demo session, you'll probably wind up with cassettes or open-reel copies of your mixes. But if you're making record albums or singles, you'll be at least briefly exposed to the disc-mastering process.

In disc mastering, the two-track tape you mixed down to in the studio will be played back at the disc cutter's through a small console similar to the one in the recording studio. The outputs of this console are connected to the inputs of the cutting lathe. The electrical signal stored on the tape will be converted into mechanical movements of the cutter's head and stylus, which will then cut grooves in a flat, shiny, lacquer-coated disc.

When a successful lacquer has been cut, it's sent to a plating plant where, metal impressions of the master lacquer are made, resulting in parts called *master*, *mother*, and *stamper*. The stamper, the last step in the process before the finished record, is attached to a press which molds the final vinyl product to fit its grooves. If the record is to be a large run (thousands of copies), several or many stampers will have to be made from the "mother" and shipped to different pressing plants around the country. The plating plant always sends its finished product out to a pressing plant. There the records are physically pressed on vinyl, labeled, inserted into paper or polyethylene sleeves, and collated into record jackets.

The record producer is generally involved with the music at least as far as the final mix of the master tape. Some producers will continue along with the process to the mastering studio where the lacquer is actually cut, and work with the mastering engineer (disc cutter). The producer may request a "reference acetate," which is an exact copy of the master lacquer, to approve before the master is sent out for plating, or in some cases, before it's even cut. Usually at this point, the producer's job is finished in terms of the physical making of the record. Unless there's a specific problem of quality that can't be handled by the quality-control people at the record label or the pressing plant, the producer can now go back to the record company and start hollering about promotional money for the act he recorded.

Studer playback decks at Master-disk Studios, N.Y.C.

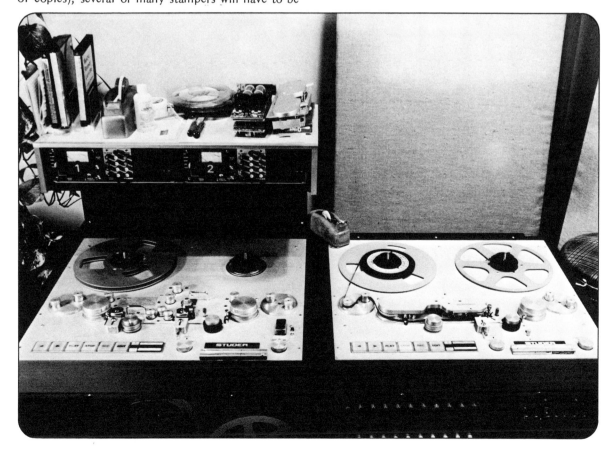

Console at Masterdisk Studios, N.Y.C.

CUTTING THE LACQUER

The actual process of transferring the master tape to the lacquer can be as simple as aligning the playback tape-machine and picking out a good lacquer-blank. In such cases, the disc cutter just plays back the tape, starts up the cutting lathe, and waits till the record's over. Many, many records are cut this way. The premise is that if it sounded great in the studio after you mixed it, then we don't want to fool around with what you did. As is frequently the case, however, several things can be done during the disc-cutting process.

It's possible that some of the songs were mixed at a different studio from some of the others. Because the monitoring situations might have been different, or because the two-track masters were mixed at slightly different levels, it may be necessary to compensate for these differences as late as the cutting ses-

sion. The disc cutter's console and outboard equipment usually include several different types of equalizers, filters, and stereo limiters. Before the lacquer is actually cut, the engineer will usually listen to the entire program on a projected side of a record to determine comparative levels, sudden peaks, and overall sound. He may do things or make suggestions that will result in the overall side's sounding more consistent. If you're new at making a master tape, you may have inadvertently caused yourself a problem or two during mixing that will require this kind of help. Disc-cutting engineers can work wonders with equalization and limiting. Don't forget that they must equalize or limit the *entire program* of a song, not just the bass drum, the vocal, or whatever else you want to change. At this stage, you're affecting the sound of the entire mix, so be careful. There are basically three ways to work a mastering session:

1. Hand in the tape and specify that the lacquer be

Disc cutting lathe at Masterdisk, N.Y.C.

cut flat. This means that the engineer won't introduce any limiting or equalization beyond what's absolutely needed to get the music on a record without skipping.

2. Hand in the tape and ask the engineer to make it sound as good as he can. This will work well in many cases, but blind trust is best given after some experience with that cutting engineer. What he thinks is great may not be what you think is great.

3. Arrange to be present for the cutting session, and work with the disc cutter the way you did with the studio engineer . . . give and take. The mastering studio will charge extra for you to be present, but if you have any questions or doubts, it's worth it to spend the extra money. After you've put at least several thousand dollars into a tape recording, it pays to spend a couple hundred extra to ensure that your lacquer is made the way you want it.

A few pointers: Monitoring in a disc-cutting room presents the same potential problems as monitoring anywhere else. What is "standard" or average? Disc-cutting studios are no more perfect listening environments than control rooms of studios. A reference acetate is recommended. Everyone wants his record to be cut as "hot" as possible. The cutter knows this and will take the appropriate steps. Don't make the sides on your album unreasonably long. Although you can comfortably record up to 28 minutes of stereo (or thereabouts) on one side of a disc, less is better. The less time there is on a side, the wider the groove width can be. This permits cutting with higher levels and reducing the possibility of "groove echo," which sounds a lot like print-through on a tape . . . it's that sound of hearing the music before you actually hear the *music.*

If you're doing pop, disco, or any kind of generally commercial music, you want to minimize the out-of-phase component in your master tape. Out-of-phase information causes vertical movement of the cutting stylus, and if it's severe enough, can present tracking problems on the record. Without getting too technical: you can "view" a mix on an oscilloscope while you're doing it to see how much out-of-phase is present. The mixing engineer should be able to hook up the scope and explain it to you. In classical music, a certain amount of out-of-phase is expected, due to the nature of the acoustical situation—big hall, reflected sound, different arrival times of direct vs. reverberant sound—but then, classical records don't need to be cut as "hot" as popular discs.

Assuming you've mixed your master tape, taken it to the disc cutter, heard a "ref" (reference acetate) and a test pressing sent from the pressing plant, you're finished. Hopefully, everything sounds great and the record is doing what you want it to do.

Beware of the following, though: Test-pressings, while they are supposed to be "samples" of the final product, are often superior to the final product in terms of surface-noise level and freedom from pressing defects. Test pressings actually verify the integrity of the metal mother and stamper from which they were made. After you've approved a test-pressing, several things can still go wrong. The holes in the record could be off center, you may hear little ticks and pops or buzzes during the music, and a higher overall level of surface-noise. If the pressing plant is clearly at fault, they will usually make good for a batch of discs. Sometimes, though, they'll blame the plating plant, who in turn blames the disc cutter, who sends the responsibility back to the plating plant. You can trace problems back as far as the metal mother, the only playable metal part, to see if your problems occurred in the mother or the stampers. In this case, if a defective stamper is indicated, new ones can be easily made. Mostly, though, the record pressing process is difficult and imperfect. Only enormous financial muscle can force a pressing plant to do better work. The other choice is to choose a *highly* reputable plant to begin with. They will charge more per pressing, and will sometimes use hand-operated presses instead of automatic, but they're frequently worthwhile for limited runs.

Unfortunately, most pressings made in the U.S. as of this writing are only poor to adequate in quality. Labels that demand excellent quality frequently send their lacquers to Japan or to Europe to be pressed. Without getting into an elaborate discussion of the situation (which is ongoing in the industry), suffice it to say that, for the moment, American pressings are basically disappointing.

11 The Future is Here

AUTOMATED MIXING

The steady growth in the number of recorded tracks from mono to 2, 3, 4, 8, 16, 24, 32, 48, and (yes, Virginia) even 64 tracks has necessitated the development of a computer-assisted mixing system. In an "ordinary" mix of, let's say, 16 tracks, the engineer's hands are usually enough to accomplish any real-time changes that have to be made in level, eq, panning, or echo during the course of a mix. Sometimes in 16- or 24-track mixing, the producer and/or assistant engineer is called upon to lend a pair of hands to push buttons on or off, fade out an overdub, or turn down the echo-send on a certain track.

As the technology became available to automate the process, recording studios began to take advantage of it. The main problem with the "hands-on" method is that it's very difficult to duplicate time after time. If the first printing of a mix goes well, but the producer wants to change a small part in the middle of the song, the engineer usually has to go through the whole complicated process of on/off, up/down all over again. Automation has put an end to some of that hassle. Level settings of individual faders, including shutting off (muting) unused tracks, and sometimes equalization settings, echo, and panning settings, can be entered into a computer memory and stored on tape or disc. When the proper settings have been entered, the engineer just plays back the mix. If the producer wants to change one small item, the engineer can "update" the computer information regarding that change. For example: suppose you have a "perfect" mix entered into the computer, but on playback it seems that the bass needs to come up during the bridge. The engineer can "write" a new program for the bass track into the computer mix simply by playing back the tape once more while he adjusts the new levels.

An additional benefit of computer mixing is the ability to recall mixes at a later date. If you go back to your multi-track master a year later to remix a "best of" album, for example, you may be hard pressed to recreate the sound you got on the original recording. With the computer information stored on the tape, you can recreate it in a matter of minutes, update to any changes you might want to make, remix it, and be out the door in a short time. Computer mixing can be a wonderful tool for making complicated mixes easier. Some engineers don't like to work with it, because the computers sometimes have their own problems, or because they think they're not "on top" of the mix if a computer is between them and the music. But computers are obviously here, and will get better and more sophisticated as time passes. There are several different automation systems available in recording studios, including those by MCI, Neve, Harrison, and Allison. They're all different from each other, but they all do the job. If you have a chance to do a computer mix, it's fascinating to get into.

MULTI-MACHINE RECORDING AND SYNC-LOC

It sometimes happens in a big budget recording that 24 tracks just aren't enough to satisfy the needs of the project. If you've gone beyond the stage of bouncing tracks, and all the unnecessary items have been eliminated (do we really need three tracks of shakers?) and you still need more tracks, one solution is to sync two multi-track machines together. This is done by interconnecting the drive motors of the two machines. In this way, both machines can be made to respond to a single "command." A very popular system for running two machines together is the SMPTE system (pronounced "simptee"), which prints a "time code" on one track of the tape, and requires the two machines to match up their respective time-code information, assuring their synchronization. Although SMPTE hardware is getting more popular every day, it represents a large investment for studios in additional equipment, so don't expect to see it at the neighborhood demo facility just yet. But if you're planning to work in a situation where it looks like more than 24 tracks might be required, sync-loc is something to ask about.

One well-prepared engineer/producer I know prefers to interlock two 16-track machines rather than two 24-tracks, because 16-tracks have a wider signal-to-noise ratio, and he feels the 30-track musical capacity is plenty. (Remember, he's using 2 tracks for the time code.) Another technique using sync-loc is to record basic tracks on the first machine, copy them onto the second machine, add the overdubs on the second machine, and transfer them back to the first machine as they're finished. The benefit of this technique is to save the basic tracks from being played back across the heads too many times. Many people believe that excessive playbacks (like in an overdub situation) of any given tape will result in deterioration of the high-frequency end of the music. For general purposes, however, you may assume that it is safe to overdub using the same machine and tape on which you recorded your basic tracks. Thousands of records have been made this way with success.

DIGITAL RECORDING

You've probably heard the term "digital recording," but you may still not be too familiar with its meaning. First, let me explain that all the recording we've dealt with up until now is know as "analog" recording. That is, the traditional type of recording, which involves storing analog magnetic signals on magnetic tape, where the music makes an electromagnetic "impression" on the tape analagous (!) to the music in terms of frequency and amplitude.

Digital recording takes the same music from the outputs of the console, but instead of registering those impressions on the tape as a rearrangement of the iron oxide particles, it converts them to numerical values through an Analog-to-Digital Converter (A/D converter), and stores those numerical values on the tape. These numbers are then retranslated at the output of the recorder through a Digital-to-Analog Converter (D/A converter) back into recognizable audio signal. So what's the difference? Simply this: With analog recordings, those magnetic impressions on the tape are subject to deleterious factors such as tape hiss, wow and flutter, distortion, and print-through. True, good analog tape recorders in good studios are finely aligned, and proper recording techniques will minimize distortions and print-through, but not to the extent available through digital recording. The digital process, since it converts the musical values to digital (binary) numbers, makes the information completely safe from those harmful factors. Since the numbers are simple "ons" and "offs," or ones and zeroes rather than complex musical waveforms, they can pass over the recording heads as if they had little blinders on, paying no attention to tape hiss, wow and flutter, distortion, and print-through.

The freedom from distortion and tape hiss, which is the hallmark of digital recording, has made it a natural for classical recording, with its extremely wide dynamic range. Classical labels, both major and independent, have in the last year begun to jump on the digital bandwagon with tremendous enthusiasm. In addition to offering a superior original recording, digital recordings can be duplicated hundreds or thousands of times with no loss of quality from the original. Further, although they cost somewhat more to produce, digital albums sell for almost twice as much as "regular" albums, a factor that is not lost on commercial enterprises such as record companies. There's been some use of digital recordings in the pop-music field, but with mixed reactions. Although it will continue to be used, and in fact grow and grow, early experiments proved, in some cases, to be un-

satisfactory to the artists involved. One artist commented that the sound was "clean, but too clean" for his ears. He had undoubtedly become accustomed to that certain amount of distortion almost always present in the traditional analog recording.

Most recording studios seem to feel that digital is not yet perfected, and with the systems ranging in price from about $30,000 to $250,000 for one or two tape recorders, they'd prefer to wait a couple of years before making the investment.

One major problem with digital technique at the moment is editing. It's not like analog tape, which can be cut with a razor blade and pasted back together. Digital edits are made with two machines and an editing console and are, at the moment much more time consuming that analog edits. This will change rapidly however, and as it does, all-digital recording, mixing, and editing projects will become more and more popular.

In a situation where one is recording "live" on location, and where only simple-to-moderately-difficult edits will need to be made, the Soundstream and Sony PCM 1600 systems are excellent. In the studio, only 3M has a full multi-track digital recorder, with 32 tracks available on 1" tape. The Sony and Soundstream systems may be used for mixing analog multi-track masters to digital, however, as can 3M's companion two- or four-track machine. I was fortunate to have participated in the first classical digital recordings to be made in New York early in 1979. The experience was fascinating and there was lots of fanfare in the press. The recordings were widely acclaimed when they were released, and I've gone on to do subsequent recordings with a number of different systems. Frankly, I'm a fan of digital recording; but to be honest, I still think a well-made analog recording can sound just as quiet and problem-free. I'd bet that not one listener in a hundred would be able to tell the difference between analog and digital tapes in most cases. Nonetheless, prototype and experimental units are being developed by JVC, Panasonic, Sony, Studer, Matsushita, and several other international companies, and as soon as the world agrees on certain standards for digital recording and editing, you're going to see a lot more of digital.

DIRECT-TO-DISC

Like digital, direct-to-disc recording has become popular in the last couple of years. Direct-to-disc records are also more expensive than "normal." records because of their superior quality and because they are more costly to make. The advantage of direct-to-disc recording is that (like digital) there's no analog tape recorder, and hence no tape recorder hiss, wow, or flutter.

Direct-to-disc was, in fact, the way all records were made before the use of magnetic tape became popular after World War II. All those old Louis Armstrong records and Bessie Smith and Enrico Caruso records were done "live." But in those days, they could only record one song at a time. The distinct disadvantage of direct-to-disc is that the *entire side of a record* must be made in real time, complete with pauses between songs. Extraneous noises or bad notes can't be edited out or "fixed in the mix." Thus, it's theoretically possible to have a great performance that lasts 17 minutes ruined by a cough at the end from one of the musicians. If that happens, it's back to square one. In addition to human errors, it's possible that the particular lacquer chosen for the recording may have a subtle defect in it. These factors tend to make the medium uncomfortable for most musicians. No one wants to play through the whole side of

a record two, three, or more times when the use of tape (analog or digital) would permit much more personal and artistic freedom. The proponents of direct-to-disc say that it produces a representation of the music superior to digital; but I've yet to be convinced.

Decisions about recording a project direct-to-disc or digital will involve discussions with record company executives, so if you'd like to record with either of these media, you'll get plenty of input before it actually happens. In a few words, if you want to go digital, do it . . . but go easy on the edits. If you want to go direct-to-disc, do it . . . but work with extremely patient musicians and bring plenty of Valium.

Glossary

A/D Converter, an electronic device which converts analog waveforms to binary numbers for digital recordings.

Analog delay, electronic device which delays audio signal without conversion to digital form by using a "bucket brigade" integrated circuit.

Audio signal, any signal within the range of human hearing, roughly from 20Hz to 20kHz; signal destined for listening, as opposed to sync signal, video signal, rf signal.

Azimuth, relationship in degrees between the gap on a tape head and tape which passes over that head.

Baffles, standing, moveable panels, either absorbent or reflective; used to create isolation between musical instruments.

Band-pass filter, electronic device to limit response above and below a given band of frequencies; opposite of notch filter.

Bias-current, high frequency signal used in tape recording to minimize distortion; normally at least 5 times the frequency of the highest audio signal.

Bi-directional microphone, a microphone with a figure-eight shaped directivity pattern with sharp nulls at 90° off normal axis.

Bouncing tracks, process of mixing prerecorded tracks and re-recording them on to an empty track for the purpose of freeing space for additional recording by overdubbing.

Bus (also buss), a signal path to which one or more inputs may be connected to feed any number of outputs.

Bus assignment, the assignment of an input or a series of input signals to a channel feeding the tape recorder. For example, the electric bass may be assigned to channel 1 during the bus assignment.

Cables, any signal-carrying conductor. Cables are used to interconnect any audio or electronic components.

Calibration controls, adjustments on a tape recorder for level, frequency response, and bias.

Calibration tones, sine wave tones which appear at the beginning of a reel of recorded tape. They are used to align the equipment to industry standards.

Cans, (jargon) earphones or headsets.

Cardioid, pertaining to microphones, a heart-shaped directivity pattern very commonly used in studio recording.

Channel, a signal path which is isolated from other signal paths such as right and left channels in a stereo system, or 24 channels (tracks) on a multi-track recorder.

Channel-send circuits, the "busses" in a recording console. They are the routes along which signal is fed to tape recorder.

Click-track, a track of tape used to store "clicks" from a digital metronome., which is used to set tempos and to time segments of music in film track recording.

Compressor, electronic device used to reduce the dynamic range of a given program or input signal.

Condenser microphone, a microphone system which translates acoustic signal (sound) into electrical signals by means of a variable capacitor.

Console, basically, a routing, amplifying and processing device for audio signals; also known as a "board," mixing console or recording desk.

Contractor, a musician who is hired to employ other musicians on behalf of the producer or record company. Contractors also prepare union contracts and paperwork associated with the employment of the musicians.

Cue, (jargon) refers, most commonly, to the headphone circuit which is fed to the musicians in the studio; also an indication to perform at a specific time (don't miss your cue); also a segment of music for film (Cue #12 is the car chase).

Cue mix, audio signal heard in headsets by musicians while recording.

Cue send, refers to the volume pot and/or circuit which feeds musicians' headsets.

Cut button, a switch (button) which is used to mute an input signal on the console.

D/A Converter, electronic device which converts binary numbers stored on tape back into continuous analog waveforms. (see *A/D Converter*)

dbx, trademark for a manufacturer of a popular noise reduction system used in recording.

DDL, digital delay line; similar in effect to analog delay, except uses digital circuitry (conversion) to achieve its effect.

Decay time, abbreviated RT60; time required (in seconds) for a sound to die away to a level of 60 decibels below it's initial peak.

Diaphragm, a membrane in a speaker system or microphone.

Digital delay line, see *DDL.*

Digital metronome, electronic device used to generate audible clicks used in film scoring and jingles. Digital metronome is calibrated in frames (of film).

Digital recording, a new recording technique which stores analog waveforms in their digital equivalents on tape or disc.

Digital reverberation, artificial reverberation device using only electronic means to create its effect.

Direct box, a small, portable box containing a transformer; used to convert signals from an electric (electronic) musical instrument to a level acceptable to studio microphone lines.

Direct-to-disc, original technique developed by Thomas Edison for recording sound on a cylinder, later a wax disc. Nowadays, an "audiophile" recording technique bypassing the use of tape recorders.

Disc-mastering, process of transferring master tape to a lacquer disc. The first step in turning a tape into a finished record.

Dolby, trademark of a widely-used noise reduction system.

Down time, (jargon) time when you're in the studio to record and equipment is out of order and/or being serviced. You are not charged for down time in a studio.

Dynamic microphone, a microphone system converting acoustic signal into electrical signal by means of a coil moving in a magnetic field.

Echo chamber, (jargon) actually, a reverberation chamber, a live room, or an electronic device used to add reverberant sound to "dry" signal recorded in the studio.

Echo-plate, specifically, an electro-mechanical device used to simulate natural reverberation.

Echo-send, the circuit or bus used to send signals from the console to the echo chamber(s).

EMT, trademark for a manufacturer of a widely-used echo plate as well as other electronic devices.

EQ, (jargon) abbreviation for equalization.

Equalization, selective modification of frequency response of an audio signal by means of selector switches and potentiometers.

Equalizer, a series of variable filters that alter frequency response.

Expander, opposite of compressor. (see *Compressor*).

Fader, (jargon) volume control, either a slider or rotary pot; used to control amplitude of audio signals.

Fade-out, gradual diminution of signals using a fader.

Filter, electronic device to boost or cut a given frequency or band of frequencies. A component part of an Equalizer. Usually used for removing unwanted signals from extreme ends of the frequency spectrum.

Flanging, similar to phasing; an electronic effect. Term originates by engineers slowing down the speed of a tape by placing a finger on the flange of a reel of tape. The characteristic sound of flanging is produced in part by "comb" filtering of the processed signal.

Flutter, cyclical pitch variation caused by mechanical imperfections in a tape or turntable drive mechanism.

Four-gang fader, fader which controls four levels simultaneously; frequently, the "master fader" at the output of a console.

Frequency response, amplitude variation within a given frequency range. For example, plus or minus ¼dB from 20Hz - 20kHz.

Gobos, (jargon) derived from the words "go between." (see *Baffles*)

Graphic Equalizer, an equalizer which covers the entire audio spectrum using one-octave to one-third octave filters in sequence.

High-fidelity, term used to describe highly accurate sound recording or reproduction.

High speed transport, tape recorder advancing tape at 15 inches per second or more.

Hypercardioid, microphone directivity pattern similar to cardioid with more acute directivity.

Input, entry point of an electronic signal into a recording or processing device; opposite of output.

Input module, module containing amplifiers, equalizers, faders, filters, cue send, etc.; as opposed to an output module which contains usually just a fader and its associated amplifier.

Jack bay, (jargon) a.k.a. patch bay; system of jacks used to interconnect component parts of console to each other or to outboard equipment. A jack bay or patch bay uses patch cords to make the interconnection.

Level, amplitude of an audio signal.

Level setting, optimizing amplitude of an audio signal for a given application.

Low-fidelity, opposite of high fidelity; a highly subjective term.

Magnetic tape master, finished, mixed master recording used for transfer to master lacquer.

Microprocessor, "brain" or control section usually on one IC (integrated circuit) chip of a small computer. Microprocessors are used in automated mixing and in sophisticated digital outboard equipment.

Mixer position, a sitting and listening position in the control room usually taken by the mixer or engineer approximately forming one apex of an equilateral triangle with the two monitor speakers.

Monitor, in audio; a quality-assessing loudspeaker used in control rooms.

Monitor echo, echo or reverberation which appears in the monitor speakers but is not printed on the tape with the "dry" audio signal.

Monitor level, acoustic level of control room speakers.

Monitor pots, level controls pertaining to monitor speakers and amps.

Monitor select, a panel of switches which determines the source of the signal being monitored. e.g., 2-track, 24-track, phono, auxiliary, echo return, etc.

Mother, a metal part in the record plating process from which stampers are made. The mother is playable on a turntable because like the finished record, it is a negative image.

Multi-track recorder, a tape recorder with greater than one track (mono) capability. Usually a 16- or 24-track recorder.

Near-field monitoring, a listening technique or condition where direct sound from loudspeakers predominates reflected sound, dependent upon distance, absorption coefficient of the room, and the directivity characteristics of the speakers.

Non-directional microphone, see *Omnidirectional*.

Notch filter, (jargon) electronic device used to remove unwanted sounds in a specific frequency band with minimal interference to surrounding frequencies.

Noise gate, electronic device which turns off audio signal below a user-set threshold.

Noise reduction, a compressing/expanding system which treats signal during record and playback in complementary manner. (see *Dolby* and *dbx*)

Off-axis, any deviation from perpendicularity (in degrees) from a microphone or loudspeaker.

Omindirectional, pertaining to microphones; the absence of a specific pickup pattern such as cardioid or bi-directional. Omni mikes are equally sensitive to signals arriving from all directions.

Open-reel, reel-to-reel tape format, as opposed to cassette and cartridge.

Outboard, (jargon) refers to external signal processing equipment; usually found in an equipment rack.

Out-of-phase, polarity reversal of one signal relative to an identical second signal causing cancellation of some frequencies.

Output, opposite of input.

Overdub, the addition of new musical or spoken material to pre-existing tracks on the same tape.

Pad, resistive circuit used to reduce signal amplitude. Pads are commonly used between the microphone and the console input.

Panning, localization of a mono signal within the 180° stereo arc; also, the act of physically moving the signal across the arc by means of a panpot.

Panpot, literally, panoramic potentiometer. (see *Panning*)

Parametric equalizer, similar to conventional equalizers, except that the parameters of frequency and bandwith are continuously variable as opposed to stepped.

Patch bay, see *Jack bay*.

Patch cord, cord (cable) to interconnect different points within a console or between console and outboard equipment via the patch bay.

Phantom powering, method of powering condenser microphones by sending DC signal over audio lines. Can be from 6 to 48 volts.

Phaser, electronic signal processing device which creates a sort of "jet plane" or swishing effect in signal introduced to its input.

Phone cable, either a two or three conductor cable with a phone (telephone) type plug at either end.

Pickup patterns, pertaining to microphone directional characteristics. Either cardioid, hypercardioid, bi-directional or omni-directional.

Pitch-change device, electronic device which alters the pitch of an input signal without changing the time relationships.

Plating, a process of electroplating used to make interim metal parts in manufacturing records.

Pot, (jargon) short for potentiometer. A variable resistor used to control amplification.

Preamp, abbreviation for preamplifier; a high gain, low noise amplifier used for microphones and other low level devices.

Pre-post switch, usually found in consoles with respect to echo send circuit. *Pre* means that the echo send enters the circuit before the fader. *Post* means that the echo send follows the fader.

Presence, the distance between the performer and the microphone. In equalization however, presence is "boosted" by adding eq around the 1-3kHz area.

Print-through, phenomenon which occurs in magnetic recording when very loud signal is followed or preceded by silence or a relatively quiet passage. Particularly noticeable with extra-thin tape.

Punch in, (jargon) to record a brief passage on an already-recorded track. For example, if an overdub is good except for the ending, you might "punch in" a new ending by engaging the tape machine in "record" mode when the ending comes up.

Radio frequency, frequencies above the audio range which are used in wireless communications. Sometimes RF (jargon) is picked up in studios when too many taxicabs with radios are in the neighborhood.

Reference acetate, lacquer disc which has been equalized and limited (or not) the way the master lacquer was, or is intended to be. Used to "preview" what a record will sound like, and as a check against possible defects in later steps of record manufacturing.

"REGEN" control, a control knob found on many delay lines which feeds the output of the device back to its own input, thereby creating an endless loop of the effect.

Remote controller, a series of function or transport controls which enable the user to operate a piece of equipment (tape recorder) from a distance.

Reproduce head, playback head on a tape recorder.

Reverberation, reflections of a sound within a room. May be artificially introduced by the use of reverberation (or echo) chambers. (see *Decay time*)

RF, RFI, see *Radio frequency.*

Ribbon microphone, a microphone in which the generating element is a metal foil ribbon suspended in an intense magnetic field.

Ring modulator, a signal processing device found in many synthesizers.

Roll-off, a filtering process usually found at extremes of the audio spectrum. May be found in microphones and equalizers.

Rough mix, any mix you take home from the studio that doesn't sound final. Rough mixes are frequently done after rhythm sessions to give the arranger a more complete idea of how the song should sound before it's finalized.

Scratch vocal, usually the vocal performance which is sung during the rhythm session. Most often, a separate session is done with the vocalist only in order to get the best possible performance. Sometimes scratch vocals do make it through to being finals.

Sel-sync, Ampex's term for selective synchronization. Enables overdubbing without a time lag, because prerecorded tracks are monitored from the record head.

Slate, term derived from the movie industry's use of a held up slate board to indicate the beginning of a new "take." Slate in recording is the engineer's voice plus a low frequency (30-40Hz) printed on the tape to indicate the song title and/or take number.

Sound-pressure level, (SPL) acoustic energy expressed in terms of decibels.

Splice, the joining of two pieces of recorded tape.

Splicing tape, special adhesive tape used for holding splices together.

Stamper, the last metal part before the final vinyl.

Stereo cue, a headphone circuit for musicians which delivers two discrete channels of information to a stereo headset as opposed to a MONO cue, which delivers the same information to both ears.

Stereo limiters, a pair of matched limiters which operate together so that both channels of a stereo tape or disc are limited at the same rate.

Stereo synthesizer, electronic device that lends spatial enchancement to old mono recordings.

Strobe tuner, a visual tuning device for musical instruments. Indicates whether they are sharp, flat, or in tune.

Supercardioid, A similarly narrow pattern. (see *Hypercardioid*)

Sweetening, the addition of string and horn parts to a rhythm track in pop music.

Sync-lock, the interlocking of two or more tape recorders, video machines, or film devices using a common sync signal.

Take, term used to indicate individual performances of a piece of music or speech; e.g., "Stairway to the Stars," Take #12.

Talkback, the circuit used for communication between control room and studio, headsets, and tape machine.

Tape hiss, broadband noise of random distribution inherent in analog tape recording. Hiss is greatly reduced by the use of a noise reduction system.

Tape slap, delaying the first repetition of a reverberated signal by over 100 milliseconds by using the distance between the record and reproduce heads of a tape recorder.

Time-code, a language used to indicate relative positions of two or more machines. Time code is printed on one track of tape. (see *Sync-lock*)

Trim pots, internal controls on tape recorder to optimize noise, frequency response, and distortion characteristics of tape and recorder.

Two-gang fader, see *Four-gang fader.*

VU meter, abbreviation of Volume Unit meter. Measuring device used in recording and broadcasting to indicate average amplitude levels relative to a standard.

XLR, most widely-used type of connector in audio work utilizing from three to seven pins.

Index

More for the Recording Musician

MIDI FOR MUSICIANS

by Craig Anderton

Finally. . .a comprehensive book that takes the mystery out of MIDI (Musical Instrument Digital Interface) once and for all. If you've been confused by the hype, the myths, and the lack of easily-understood information, this book tells you how and why MIDI can open up new musical vistas for you - no matter what instrument you play. MIDI is a revolutionary concept, one that will have far-reaching impact on the way we play, compose, record, distribute, and even transcribe music. If you've been wondering what all the fuss is about, look no further - the answers are in those pages.

Order No. AM 61219
ISBN 0.8256.1050.8

ELECTRONIC DRUMS

by Frank Vilardi with Steve Tarshis

This is *the* indispensible guide to electronic drum kits and drum computers; what to look for when purchasing, how they work, the ins and outs of programming them. Includes comprehensive reviews of all the leading names, from the earliest Syndrum to the state-of-the-art Linn 9000; a basic guide to song programming; plus a demonstration soundsheet showing how 'analog' drums, electronic drums, and drum computers can be combined to add excitement and color to your musical projects.

Order No. AM 37342
ISBN 0.8256.2440.1

ELECTRONIC PROJECTS FOR MUSICIANS
REVISED EDITION

by Craig Anderton

This revised edition is perfect for thrifty and creative musicians. There are chapters on how to build preamps, tone controls, ring modulators, mixers and many other inexpensive accessories, even without prior electronic aptitude. It is written in simple language, with hundreds of clear illustrations and easy step-by-step instructions, including a six minute demonstration record. This edition has been updated and expanded with many new projects. Foreword by Joe Walsh.
Order No. AM 32707
ISBN 0.8256.9502.3

GUITAR GADGETS

by Craig Anderton

This 'consumer guide' written by *the* expert on the subject of outboard signal processing devices. Covers the proper use and theory behind such 'little black boxes' as digital and analog delays, tape echo, distortion units, noise gates, graphic and parametric equalizers in easy to understand everyday language. Includes valuable pointers on how to shop for devices; what 'quality points' to look for, and if something goes wrong, how to troubleshoot for common defects that can save you money and aggravation. Includes a free demonstration soundsheet. Not for guitarists only! You keyboard players out there can really benefit from this book also!
Order No. AM 34174
ISBN 0.8256.2214.X

THE DIGITAL DELAY HANDBOOK

by Craig Anderton

Written by *the* expert on electronics as applied to music, this outstanding book contains 69 different applications, suitable for a variety of instruments, which help you unlock the hidden potential in virtually any delay line. Whether live or in the studio, this handbook helps you to create signal processing magic with one of the most popular and commonly available effects.
Order No. AM 38985
ISBN 0.8256.2414.2

YAMAHA DX7 DIGITAL SYNTHESIZER

by Yasuhiko Fukuda

A thoroughly comprehensive manual, containing everything you need to know for successful operation of the DX7. As well as covering the basic mechanism and operation, it contains the functional explanations for more advanced sound making techniques. Also describes procedures for editing and tone creation.
Order No. AM 39371
ISBN 0.7119.0653.X

HOME RECORDING FOR MUSICIANS

by Craig Anderton

Everything one needs to know to make good, clear, professional-sounding recordings at home, using affordable equipment, is in this book. Topics extensively covered include tape decks, microphones, studio equipment, tape, audio theory, noise reduction, acoustics, and studio environment. There are many clear diagrams and simple illustrations plus a demonstration soundsheet.
Order No. AM 32699
ISBN 0.8256.9501.5

HOW TO MAKE AND SELL YOUR OWN RECORD

THE COMPLETE GUIDE TO INDEPENDENT RECORDING

by Diane Sward Rappaport

Every aspect of a recording project is covered in this unique guide: setting up a studio, finding musicians, mixing and editing a record, pressing the record, and designing the cover. Plus information on copyrights, licensing and royalties, and hints on sales, promotion and advertising.
Order No. HE 10000
ISBN 0.399.51092.3